To my late friend Gian Battista Bozzato.
May this book honor your memory.

Published by Actitudes Coaching – Frederic Meuwly
Actitudes Coaching
Rue des Communaux 35
1800 Vevey
Switzerland
www.actitudescoaching.com

Printed and distributed by IngramSpark in the United States and Canada, United Kingdom and Europe, Australia, and New Zealand.

Legal copy deposit available from the Swiss National Library:
Swiss National Library
Hallwylstrasse 15
3003 Berne
Switzerland
ISBN 978-2-9701418-7-7 (paperback)

Editor: Richard Eames
Design and illustrations: David Picard

The diagram on page 23 is reproduced with the kind permission of Marco Mancesti.

Welcome!

I am glad you are here.

Reading a book is like going on a journey with its author. As you travel through the following pages, I hope you will find many useful nuggets to put in your backpack.

I begin by describing how my own personal and professional journey has shaped my approach to developing teams and organizations. Having outlined the key concepts and guiding principles, I then share many of the practical tools that my colleagues and I use to help leaders transform their teams into what I call *sustainable teams*.

The book includes three real-world case studies showing how different organizations have used the 18 team sustainability drivers to improve performance. The final section contains tips regarding best practices and things to avoid for each driver, which I hope will serve as a helpful go-to reference.

While some of the ideas and examples in this book may mirror your own team development efforts, others may lead to fresh insights that you can share with your colleagues and wider network.

But even after 20 years of research, team leadership experience, and practical work in the field of team coaching and organizational development, I am still learning and adapting. Maybe your team has developed other best practices that you would like me to include in future editions of this book.

If you have comments or questions about building sustainable teams, then please feel free to get in touch. You can reach me at frederic.meuwly@actitudescoaching.com.

I hope this book will inspire you and your team to identify and focus on what really matters. I hope you will discover new tools to help you successfully develop sustainable teams. Most importantly, I hope you will enjoy the journey – and let the magic of great teamwork happen!

Frederic Meuwly, Ph.D.

Foreword

By George A. Kohlrieser

Sustainable Teams is a must-read for anyone who is looking to make the miracle of great teamwork happen within their organization.

This book empowers leaders and their teams to go beyond their current routines and find the inspiration and tools they need to achieve long-term success. Fred Meuwly recognizes that leadership is a calling. What's more, he shows how sustainable teams take teamwork to another level by fully leveraging the power of collective intelligence, thus co-creating lasting value that serves a higher purpose and achieves a greater good.

Fred develops the notion of teams as complex human ecosystems that constantly interact with the forces at play within and beyond their boundaries. He makes us aware that in teams, like in other living systems, individual organs cannot function in isolation. Life can flow and pulse through the whole organism only when the different organs become interconnected and work in synergy.

The same logic underpins Fred's insightful and evidence-based approach to building sustainable teams. Like an alchemist, he has boiled down the complex systemic interactions between a team and its environment into a practical guide centered around 18 team sustainability drivers.

This framework is a key asset to help leaders, teams, and organizations successfully navigate change. It gives them a prism to see clearly through the fog, and builds a secure base that prevents them from being taken hostage by uncertainty and complexity. By focusing on these 18 drivers, teams can channel their mind's eye and concentrate their energy on what they can influence. This process encourages them to let go of their fears and "play to win" as they pursue collective goals.

As a professor of leadership and organizational behavior, I have seen thousands of leaders struggle to maintain high-performance teamwork in turbulent times. High volatility and uncertainty may destabilize teams, and make them fearful and defensive – what I call a "playing not to lose" mindset. Even the most successful teams can end up paralyzed by fear and anxiety and slide into dysfunction when unexpected changes occur.

Similarly, my work as a clinical psychologist and hostage negotiator has brought me into contact with many leaders and teams who were being held hostage – either physically or psychologically – and felt helpless and powerless. One of the keys to helping people move to a hostage-free mindset is to make them feel safe and secure so that they can let go of their defensiveness and shift their mind's eye toward options, opportunities, and creative solutions. A secure-base leader or coach can help them to channel individual and collective transformations by working with the elements of caring and daring.

This book can serve as a powerful secure base for your team. Thinking, feeling, and living as a sustainable team will transform your experience of teamwork, and act as a strong anchor that shapes your team's identity. By unlocking the best that you and your co-workers have to offer, this book will accelerate your team's development and help to unleash its full potential.

Sustainable Teams is full of practical resources and tools to catalyze the transformations needed to build great team dynamics. Fred's sustainable teams framework can serve as a safe harbor for your team to reconnect, recharge, and rejuvenate, and one that you can return to anytime you need inspiration and ideas on how to move forward.

During that journey, the 18 team sustainability drivers will give you momentum and direction. If your team risks drifting toward the dark side of teamwork, the drivers can help them to avoid toxic behaviors and shift gears to rekindle positive group dynamics. They can become part of your team's collective wisdom, and serve as a platform from which it can explore and grow in order to produce measurable and sustainable results.

I often conclude my programs by asking leaders to consider how they can apply the following advice from the nineteenth-century American writer and thinker Ralph Waldo Emerson to their leadership: "Do not go where the path may lead, go instead where there is no path and leave a trail."

This is exactly what Fred has done in this book. At a time when many organizations are still overly focused on short-term returns, *Sustainable Teams* is a vibrant call for us to redefine teamwork in response to profoundly disruptive changes in our environment, societies, and economies.

I hope that organizational leaders will dare to take their teams a step further and explore the path that will transform them into sustainable teams, so that it soon becomes a trail. If I sound excited about this book, it is because I am – and I trust that you will find it valuable, too!

December 2020

George A. Kohlrieser is Distinguished Professor of Leadership and Organizational Behavior at IMD business school in Lausanne, Switzerland. He is the author of the award-winning books *Hostage at the Table: How Leaders Can Overcome Conflict, Influence Others, and Raise Performance* (2006) and *Care to Dare: Unleashing Astonishing Potential Through Secure Base Leadership* (2012).

About this Book

This book is intended to be a resource and field guide for executives, department heads, project leaders, and specialists in talent and organizational development, such as human resources professionals, work psychologists, coaches, consultants, mediators, and ombudspersons.

DEPARTMENT HEADS

are accountable and strongly influence how each unit or team thinks, feels, and performs within their department.

EXECUTIVES

set the pace, as well as the tone of the organization's overall culture and values. They shape the context and define the standards to which leaders and teams operate.

SPECIALISTS

provide insights and guidance and sometimes facilitate best practices to develop high-performing teams and promote organizational health.

PROJECT LEADERS

are ultimately in the driver's seat. They have a direct impact on teams' morale and performance through their daily interactions with team members.

Successfully building sustainable teams within an organization requires synchronized efforts from all of these groups. Each plays a key role in the process.

Contents

PART I – The Magic of Great Teamwork

This section explains what makes sustainable teams different, highlights three key concepts underpinning them, discusses the magic of great teamwork in high-performing groups, and warns that many teams also have a dark, dysfunctional side.

Why this book?

I first got involved in different forms of teamwork as a kid – whether through competitive activities like playing soccer, or much more collaborative pursuits such as playing trumpet in the music school's orchestra. But I gained my first conscious exposure to teamwork in my early twenties, when I graduated as an engineer and started work as a junior scientist in a biotech company.

Although my initial duties were closely related to my technical and scientific skills, I soon moved into a more managerial role. For the next ten years, I focused mainly on leading different types of teams and projects, while still occasionally digging into the science.

About halfway through that period, by which time I was leading multiple cross-functional teams that were developing a number of biotech drugs, I realized how difficult it was for teams to perform on both a business and human level.

I initially thought that successful drug development involved finding a safe and effective drug that we could swiftly bring from research into clinical trials. The treatment would eventually gain approval from the relevant health authorities, come to market, and benefit its target patient population. As a recent engineering graduate, I was convinced that the golden rule was 80% product and 20% teamwork. But subsequent experience proved me wrong.

On the one hand, I noticed that some teams that had been lucky enough to inherit a great product somehow got mired in destructive dynamics. They suffered from interpersonal rivalries and conflicts, an unwillingness among several team members to share information, lack of coordination, destructive competition between different departments, and a lack of transparency on important product-quality issues. And, to be honest, my own lack of leadership skills at that early stage of my career did not help matters.

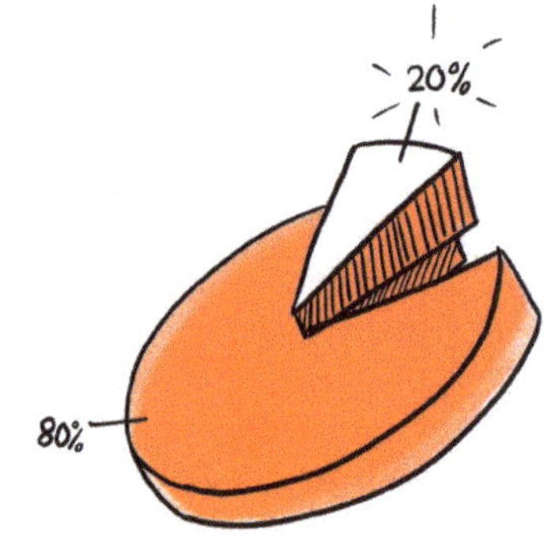

But on the other hand, I saw that other teams progressed faster despite inheriting more difficult product candidates. Instead of being delayed by the numerous scientific and technological challenges, they somehow performed better, and showed a higher level of creativity, coordination, and engagement. This prompted me to reverse my initial 80/20 rule – I was now convinced that the ideal balance was 20% product and 80% teamwork. But again, experience proved me wrong: even with great teamwork, it was sometimes impossible to overcome major product-related limitations.

That realization prompted a series of questions. I began asking myself:

● What kind of "magic" enables outstanding teams to perform on both a **business** and **human** level?

● Can we identify a few underlying **drivers** to help leaders and organizations set teams up for success?

● Similarly, can we identify the most common **traps, derailers, and indicators** in order to prevent teams from becoming dysfunctional?

● What can be done to help teams establish and then maintain, sustain, and nurture **positive team habits** and outstanding performance in the long run?

● Is there a **reliable and reproducible** way to develop teams that **create value** within their **whole ecosystem**?

These questions have been keeping me busy ever since, and form the basis of this book.

My personal journey

When I first discovered my passion for team development, I quickly realized that this was not a topic you could learn at school like mathematics, philosophy, biology, or economics. So, I started to seek different ways to gain experience and expertise in this field. I read the existing team-management literature, attended leadership and executive education programs, and trained to become a certified coach. And I tried to apply this knowledge when leading teams at the biotech firm where I worked.

Over time, I developed a personal vision of how teams could collaborate, how team members could be empowered through distributed leadership instead of a top-down approach to management, and how collective intelligence and cooperation could help to make teams more creative and effective.

My personal reflections coincided with the global rise of environmental consciousness and the emergence of new business models.
I was strongly inspired when Muhammad Yunus[1] and Grameen Bank received the 2006 Nobel Peace Prize for pioneering the concept of social businesses based on microcredit and microfinance. And crucially, the notion of sustainability started to spread from ecology into other social and entrepreneurial spheres. Global initiatives such as the World Business Council for Sustainable Development[2], the Solar Impulse Foundation[3], and the Ellen MacArthur Foundation[4]  invite us to consider sustainability through different lenses and contribute to finding new synergies between environmental, economic, and societal drivers.

I came to realize that progress could go hand in hand with sustainability, and that governments, large companies, and other organizations could be persuaded to shift toward new tools reconciling ecology and economy. What's more, I felt a kind of calling, and realized that I too could play a role in shaping this transition.

I therefore began asking myself:

● What if the concepts of sustainability, circularity, and ecosystems could also be applied to the way we develop teams and organizations?

● What if we could develop synergetic ways to apply a growth mindset that encompasses both human and business outcomes?

● What if we could rethink the way we develop products and services so that they benefit all stakeholders along an integrated value chain in the long run, instead of making unethical decisions to maximize our profits in the short term?

[1]Muhammad Yunus, Building Social Business: The New Kind of Capitalism That Serves Humanity's Most Pressing Needs, Reprint edition (New York, NY: PublicAffairs, 2011).

[2]"The Future of Work | Mobilizing Business Action to Shape a Future of Work That Enables People, Business and Societies to Thrive," https://futureofwork.wbcsd.org/.

[3]Bertrand Piccard, Solar Impulse Foundation, 1000 profitable solutions for the environment, https://solarimpulse.com/.

[4]"Circular Economy - UK, USA, Europe, Asia & South America - The Ellen MacArthur Foundation," https://www.ellenmacarthurfoundation.org/.

By 2007, I had reached a turning point. I decided then that I would break free from my current professional path and dedicate the next phase of my life and career to **applying the principles of sustainable development to leaders, teams, and organizations.**

It was clear to me *why* I was making this career shift. But it took me several months to figure out *how* I was going to inspire leaders to adopt a more sustainable vision of team and organizational development.

During that transition period, I tested my ideas with a diverse range of leaders in different organizations, sectors, and roles, including HR, workplace health management (doctors and nurses), health-safety-environment (HSE), learning and development, and business schools. Although they generally found my ideas attractive, they also said that they were not 100% clear about how to apply sustainable-development principles within their teams. They agreed with the overall intent but needed more guidance to make that change.

Disillusion, disruption, and inspiration

At around this time, my wife Susan and I had started to build a family. And, as is the case for many new parents, the birth of our first child in 2007 caused me to start questioning some of my fundamental principles. This exercise reinforced my conviction that conscious leadership – being aware of the social, economic, and ecological impact of our decisions and actions, and of their long-term effect across different systems – is essential within both a family and business context. I became much more aware of my values and business ethics, and soon realized that there were major gaps between them and the way we were developing and commercializing biotech drugs.

For several months, I could feel a growing gap between my aspirations and the reality of my context. I was trying to bridge this divide and hold everything together. But eventually, the gulf became so wide that I experienced a total disconnect. And in January 2010, I collapsed into a state of exhaustion and burnout.

That was of course a highly disruptive experience, but in hindsight it was also a big gift that changed my life. Above all, I am extremely grateful for all the support I received from family, friends, and health professionals during that time. Much later, in 2018, I gave a TEDx talk[5] in which I explained how "welcoming disruption" had been a key element of my recovery, and a necessary step to enable me to make sense of my experience and then rebound (and re-bond).

As I struggled to recover in the months following my burnout, I made a commitment to myself to practice conscious leadership in the different areas of my life. And I had known since 2007 that I wanted to start a new professional venture.

So, toward the end of 2010, I founded Actitudes Coaching with the aim of helping organizations to establish the foundations for sustainable development and performance through what I now call the **building sustainable teams** approach.

So, what makes sustainable teams special? In short, they not only build great capabilities, but also develop the capacity to sustain them over time.

---

[5]Burnout… A Friend of a Friend's Problem | Frédéric Meuwly | TEDxSHMS, https://www.youtube.com/watch?v=TTRTG7l1cV0.

SUSTAINABLE TEAMS

● consistently act in accordance with their
purpose and core values, regardless of the
turbulence in their environment

● consciously choose to **co-create value** with
all stakeholders in their ecosystem

● are always mindful of how their choices
in the present will drive **long-term** organizational
health and performance.

Sustainable teams therefore tend to outperform other
teams in terms of both results and organizational impact.

Inspirational currents

The sustainable teams concept is rooted in three currents that I have combined to create a new framework for organizational and team development.

The circular economy[6]

We are now shifting to an economic system in which we design out waste and pollution, keep products and materials in use, and regenerate natural systems.

So, I applied the same logic to the use of people and talent in organizations.

Sustainable teams aim for "zero waste" by minimizing the time and energy lost due to inefficient teamwork, including as a result of lengthy decision-making, low levels of mutual trust, destructive team conflicts, poor coordination, and lack of clarity on roles and responsibilities.

Sustainable teams consider people as whole human beings, and not just as employees or staff. This approach is the opposite of the linear economy's take-make-waste model, according to which we take resources (including people) to make products that we throw away when we no longer want them.

Through sustainable teams, organizations create value for themselves, their stakeholders, *and* the people who contribute to the organization's long-term success. The goal is to develop talents and leverage everyone's skills and contributions beyond their current role within the organization.

Design out waste and pollution   Keep products and materials in use

Regenerate natural systems

[6]Ken Webster, Dame Ellen MacArthur, and Walter Stahel, The Circular Economy: A Wealth of Flows, 2nd Edition (Cowes, Isle of Wight, United Kingdom: Ellen MacArthur Foundation Publishing, 2017).

This is a key driver of an organization's resilience, and reflects its ability to function effectively, cope adequately, change appropriately, and grow from within.

As Manfred Kets de Vries has pointed out[8], "given the importance of individual psychological well-being for effective organizational performance, leaders would be wise to create healthy places to work," or what de Vries calls "authentizotic" workplaces[9].

The goal is that employees are both inspired by the integrity of their organization's vision, mission, values, culture, and structure, and invigorated by their workplace, where they find a sense of balance and completeness.

The World Health Organization defines health as "a state of complete physical, mental, and social well-being." So, I used the same definition to gauge a team's health status and look for the factors that show whether it is in good physical, mental, and social condition.

---

[7] Patrick Lencioni, The Advantage: Why Organizational Health Trumps Everything Else In Business (John Wiley & Sons, 2012).

[8] Manfred F. R. Kets de Vries, The Hedgehog Effect: The Secrets of Building High Performance Teams (John Wiley & Sons, 2011).

[9] Manfred F. R. Kets de Vries, "The 'Authentizotic' Organization: Creating Best Places to Work," SSRN Scholarly Paper (Rochester, NY: Social Science Research Network, April 25, 2018), https://doi.org/10.2139/ssrn.3168680.

Impact models for workplace health management and employee engagement[10]

These tools are useful for demonstrating cause-effect relationships and showing the positive impact of such activities.

They help leaders to see how their spending on team development brings both tangible and intangible benefits to their organizations, enabling them to frame it as an investment that yields returns rather than as a cost.

So, I applied the same logic to show an explicit link between the efforts invested in team development and the resulting organizational outcomes. These include better business performance, increased customer satisfaction, lower personnel turnover, lower sick-leave costs, lower recruitment costs, and improved brand attractiveness and reputation – not to mention the benefits to the team itself, of course.

After I founded Actitudes, I started to work on identifying the key drivers that contribute to building sustainable teams. Then, in 2015, the United Nations launched its Sustainable Development Goals (SDGs)[11], a set of interconnected global objectives intended to bring about a better and more sustainable future for all.

I was encouraged by the parallels between the SDGs and my philosophy of building sustainable teams. And as I continued my research, the UN goals inspired me to see whether I could develop a similar, smaller-scale approach to help build more sustainable teams and organizations.

By analyzing how great teamwork gradually emerges from a group, I progressively identified **18 Team Sustainability Drivers** that simultaneously contribute to getting team members sustainably **enabled**, **energized**, and **engaged** in their work. These building blocks, which I introduce in more detail in Part III, are the essence of sustainable teams.

I then cross-checked my findings with research in the fields of team development, high-performing teams, group dynamics, organizational psychology, employee engagement, general management, talent and leadership development, living systems, sustainability, and the circular economy. This resulted in the innovative approach to team and organizational development that I am sharing with you in this book.

I progressively identified 18 Team Sustainability Drivers that simultaneously contribute to getting team members sustainably enabled, energized, and engaged in their work.

---

[10]WHM Effectiveness Review - Gesundheitsförderung Schweiz, https://healthpromotion.ch/workplace-health-management/ studien-wirkung-bgm/whm-effectiveness-review.html.

[11]Sustainable Development Knowledge Platform, https://sustainabledevelopment.un.org/.

The magic of great teamwork

Trying to achieve great teamwork is a highly fascinating and complex endeavor.

Teams essentially exist to co-create value. Their purpose is to create and deliver solutions better, faster, and more sustainably than individuals can on their own.

This does not mean that team members should suppress their individual creativity. Rather, like the colorful gems in a kaleidoscope, they should act in synergy to combine their unique abilities. The picture will probably look messy at the start, because it takes time and effort for team members to interact and collaborate in new ways. But the team will be working hard to create something beautiful and greater than the sum of its parts. And when the true magic of teamwork eventually happens, a new picture will emerge from the kaleidoscope!

In today's increasingly complex and interconnected world, we urgently need to tap into the power of collective intelligence and teamwork. In recent decades, organizations have focused a lot on leadership development. But I think there is now a pressing need to use new tools and approaches in developing *teams*, and *sustainable teams* in particular.

After all, teams are literally everywhere: in the arts, sports, volunteer work, business, government, public services, and many other areas besides. Whatever your field of activity, you are most probably engaged in some form of teamwork. And as you know, teamwork is full of wonders, but it can also be full of nightmares.

We often hear about the bright sides of teamwork, and most of us aspire to be part of an outstanding team. Groups of smart individuals frequently collaborate successfully in high-performing teams. In their book *Virtuoso Teams*[12], Andy Boynton and Bill Fischer provide several inspiring examples of the wonderful transformations that teamwork and collective intelligence can achieve.

Such great outcomes usually occur when organizations and their leaders create the right environment and context for teams to successfully mature and grow into high-performing units.

But what does a high-performing team look like? Just sit back, relax, and imagine how it would feel to be part of a team that has a clear purpose...receives 100% support from the organization's leadership...contains people who are inspired by their mission and goals... truly engages in co-creation, with everyone contributing to its success... regards trust, care, support, and empathy as the norm...is able to deal with conflicts constructively...and so on.

[12] Andy Boynton and Bill Fischer, Virtuoso Teams: The Extraordinary Stories of Extraordinary Teams (Harlow: Financial Times Prentice Hall, 2009).

Although I sincerely hope you have already experi-enced such great teamwork, I realize that the above description may sound too naive and idealistic. Most of us, after all, have also experienced disillusion and discord in teams.

Dysfunctional teams

Unfortunately, teams also have their dark sides. It does not take much to flip the coin and derail them – and when that happens, things can get very bad indeed.

As Patrick Lencioni has noted[13], team dysfunctions usually occur at different levels. They include ab-sence of trust, fear of conflict (conflict avoidance), lack of commitment, avoidance of accountability, and inattention to results.

In my own work, I am regularly called in by leaders or their HR colleagues to help them resolve challenging team dy-namics. And I am often surprised at how many leaders still use team coaching resources in a reactive way. They tend to wait until the team's challenges become pressing be-fore requesting team development activities. It's always a pity to see how much energy is being wasted in such situ-ations, and how much damage people and businesses can suffer when things start to become dysfunctional. Team dysfunctions can sometimes have irreversible impacts, and should therefore be addressed as early as possible.

To begin with, it is critical that teams learn to make sense of what is happening at different levels in the team, organizational, and external environment. To do that suc-cessfully, they need to acquire the skills to regulate their areas of tension and find creative ways to transcend their conflicts and traumas. Although team coaching can some-times be key to catalyzing such transformations, it is not an absolute remedy and has its limitations. Other trained professionals such as ombudspersons, mediators, and psychologists can also play a vital role in helping teams to unlock difficult situations, including by supervising group dynamics in a systemic way.

---

[13] Patrick Lencioni, The Five Dysfunctions of a Team: A Leadership Fable, 1st edition (San Francisco: Jossey-Bass, 2002).

Above all, working with teams requires specific skills. Coaches and other external facilitators need to be aware of a team's emotions and underlying group dynamics, and should encourage its members to maintain a sense of empathy and solidarity as they go through challenging times individually and collectively.

Of course, one could argue that tensions and conflicts are not only unavoidable, but also essential to progress. Indeed, many psychoanalytic and sociological schools of thought regard intrapsychic and extrapsychic conflicts as necessary to any form of growth, evolution, and genuine creativity.

But if such issues are left unaddressed for too long, the team will reach a tipping point beyond which it starts to drift and becomes increasingly toxic and dysfunctional. This will inevitably translate into poor performance and have a negative long-run impact on the team and its wider environment, both within and outside the organization.

To maintain a healthy balance between the bright and dark sides of teams, we need to find ways to challenge ourselves and work on our "shadow." This is the dark side of our personality that consists mostly of primitive, negative human emotions and impulses like rage, envy, greed, selfishness, desire, and the striving for power. It includes everything that we deny in ourselves (both individually and also collectively as a group, team, or organization), and whatever we perceive as inferior, evil, or unacceptable.

Introspection, supervision, and "shadow work" are crucial to keep us from dissociating from our shadow. This process enables us to reintegrate the dark (and also sometimes the positive) parts of ourselves that were previously repressed. As a result, we can express our whole self; as Carl Jung once said, "I'd rather be whole than good." Such wholeness is vital to maintaining an objective, realistic, and centered view of our (sometimes) unconscious underlying dynamics.

So, before we move to Part II, let's quickly check the quality of the teamwork in your current professional environment.

REALITY CHECK

- When in your life or career did you last experience the "magic" of true teamwork?

- Looking at your current team(s), which would you say is more visible: the "bright side" or the "dark side" of teamwork?

- How would you assess your current team dynamics, creativity, and overall performance on a scale of 1 to 10?

- Is your team able to face challenges, deal with conflict constructively, and seek opportunities through change?

- Do you feel that interpersonal or work relationships still suffer as a result of past situations and challenges being left unresolved for too long? What would it take for you and your team to re-bond, and strengthen or restore deep mutual trust and psychological safety?

- Do you feel that you and your team are living an adventure that contributes to co-creating better products, solutions, and services? Does your team's work benefit all stakeholders along your value chain as well as your wider environment?

- What would you and your team need to move forward?

Make sure you regularly take time to reflect on these questions and their implications for you, your team, and your organization.

KEY LEARNINGS

Part I

1. Sustainable teams **co-create value** with all stakeholders and are **mindful** of how their current choices will impact the organization's long-term health and performance.

2. The sustainable teams concept is rooted in three currents - the **circular economy, organizational health,** and **impact models for workplace health management and employee engagement.** I have combined these to create a new framework for team and organizational development.

3. Synchronized efforts and a **shared culture** are necessary to **set the context** that will enable your organization to successfully build sustainable teams. No matter what role you have, you can actively contribute to this process.

4. The **magic of great teamwork** happens when groups unleash the potential of collective intelligence. But **team dysfunctions** can sometimes have irreversible impacts, and should therefore be addressed as early as possible.

Capture your own

INSIGHTS

....

ACTIONS

....

THINGS TO SHARE

....

PART II – A New Paradigm for Team and Organizational Development

This section outlines the book's underlying concepts and explains why we need new models for team and organizational development in an increasingly volatile, uncertain, complex, and ambiguous (VUCA) world, where frequent and sometimes disruptive changes have become the new norm.

From linear to circular

Many traditional models of team development outline a *linear step-by-step process*, with teams requiring several successive steps to gradually develop from workgroups into high-performing units.

One classical example is Bruce Tuckman's well-known model of the developmental sequence in small groups[14], according to which teams progressively mature across successive phases of development (forming, storming, norming, performing, adjourning). Another is the Drexler-Sibbet Team Performance Model®[15] co-developed by Allan Drexler and David Sibbet, which breaks down team development into seven stages – four to create the team, and three to achieve increasing levels of sustained performance. And we typically look at change in the same way: most change-management models also take a linear step-by-step approach.

But in today's increasingly volatile, uncertain, complex, and ambiguous (VUCA) world, this linear view of team building and change management no longer works. We need to replace linear and binary thinking with concepts such as circularity, sustainability, and interdependency, and take a more systemic view of our interactions with other human beings, other species, and our wider environment.

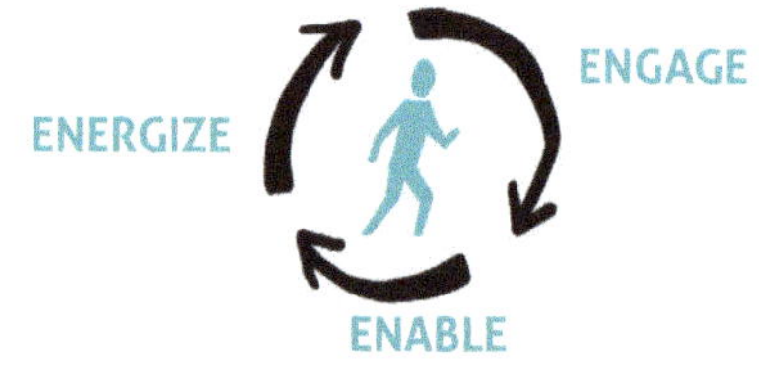

---

[14]B. W. Tuckman, "Developmental Sequence in Small Groups," Psychological Bulletin 63 (June 1965): 384–99, https://doi.org/10.1037/h0022100.

[15]David Sibbet, "Process Models," https://davidsibbet.com/process-models/.

In recent years, numerous unforeseen shocks have challenged our ecology, societies, and economies, the latest of these being the COVID-19 pandemic that has swept across the world since the beginning of 2020. The world of change management has been replaced by one where we must learn how to individually and collectively cope with and overcome profound transformations and disruptions. This is a clear signal that the old recipe does not work anymore, and a clear invitation to rethink how we work, live, and interact with ecosystems both inside and outside our organizations.

A new vocabulary has therefore emerged: Agility. Resilience. Transformation. Disruption. And these are not just buzzwords. They signify fundamental shifts in the way we live and work. We quickly need to identify new synergies, new methods of working, and new ways to interact and thrive within our environment.

What VUCA means for organizations, leaders, and teams

Adapting to today's VUCA environment requires leaders, teams, and organizations to change the way they operate. They need to build new organizational models, new leadership skills, and new approaches to organizational and team development.

New organizational models

Regardless of their previous governance model, organizations need to recreate themselves in order to thrive in a VUCA environment. Or, as Frederic Laloux argues[16], we need to "reinvent organizations and create organizations that are inspired by the next stage in human consciousness."

In general, the old command-and-control management approach characterized by vertical and hierarchical structures is making way for more circular, sociocratic governance systems and flatter structures. And since the early 2010s, several organizations have adopted the decentralized holacratic model of self-managing teams pioneered by management thinker Brian Robertson[17].

Ironically, military leaders were among the first to advocate dropping the top-down management approach, at a time when many business executives were still applying pyramidal governance principles. Former US submarine commander David Marquet's *Turn the Ship Around!*[18] and General Stanley McChrystal's *Team of Teams*[19], for instance, offer inspiring examples of how to empower teams and engage people in an increasingly complex world.

Such accounts will hopefully persuade many business leaders to instill a more participative culture into their organizations. Smart distribution of authority and decision-making power not only reduces the pressure on leaders to make every decision, but also makes teams more agile and resilient because they are more likely to respond quickly to changes in their environment.

---

[16]Frederic Laloux and Ken Wilber, Reinventing Organizations: A Guide to Creating Organizations Inspired by the Next Stage of Human Consciousness, 1st edition (Brussels: Nelson Parker, 2014).

[17]Brian J. Robertson, Holacracy: The New Management System for a Rapidly Changing World (New York: Henry Holt and Co., 2015).

[18]L. David Marquet and Stephen R. Covey, Turn the Ship Around!: A True Story of Turning Followers into Leaders, 1st edition (New York: Portfolio, 2013).

[19]Gen Stanley McChrystal et al., Team of Teams: New Rules of Engagement for a Complex World, 1st edition (New York, New York: Portfolio, 2015).

New leadership *actitudes*

The emergence of new organizational models has direct implications for how leaders need to think, feel, and behave, and act (or interact) with their team members.

In our current VUCA environment, levels of uncertainty and complexity are so high that leaders cannot manage them as they did previously. Instead, senior executives must develop new *actitudes* – and, even more importantly, they need to revisit their role and posture as leaders.

I created the word "actitudes" to illustrate how leaders' actions now have to derive from new aptitudes and attitudes. And I named my company Actitudes Coaching because the word stands for some important notions that I think should be integral to leadership today.

Throughout this book, I emphasize that appropriate leadership is a prerequisite for building successful sustainable teams. That in turn requires leaders to develop three sets of actitudes in particular.

First, leaders must become much more **conscious and connected** regarding what is happening around them. As Marco Mancesti has argued, organizations need "disruption-fit leaders" in order to survive[20]. These "top-notch sensors" can simultaneously scan three "sensing layers": the sector (the business playing field), people (all contributing teams and communities), and themselves (their inner balance).

Second, leaders need to create a climate of **psychological safety** by developing actitudes such as empathy, vulnerability, compassion, and authenticity. What we used to call mutual trust in a team has been replaced by the much deeper notion of "psychological safety," whereby team members are able to secure themselves and others despite an ever-changing and challenging environment that some may perceive as threatening. For example, Harvard Business School professor Amy Edmondson has highlighted the need to create "fearless organizations"[21], while the author Simon Sinek outlined in a famous TED talk[22] "why good leaders make you feel safe."

Finally, leaders need to become strong **"secure bases"** for themselves and their teams, a notion developed by IMD professor George Kohlrieser[23]. Fear, anxiety, and insecurity are natural reactions that can easily be triggered when we face high levels of uncertainty and complexity. Having a strong secure base can enable us to mitigate those feelings and restore an internal state in which we feel predominantly safe and secure. This will unlock our ability to

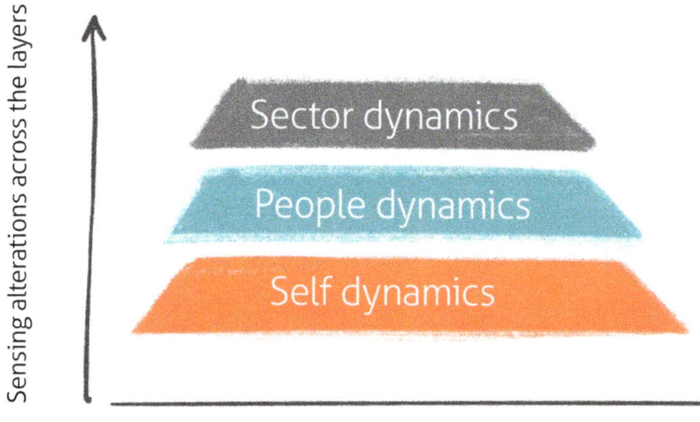

think creatively, explore challenges with a growth mindset, and seek opportunities in a changing environment. For more insights and resources on this theme, I highly recommend Kohlrieser's book *Care to Dare: Unleashing Astonishing Potential Through Secure Base Leadership.*

---

[20]Marco Mancesti, "The Disruption-Fit Leader and Why Companies Need Them to Survive," IMD business school, https://www.imd.org/research-knowledge/articles/the-disruption-fit-leader/.

[21]Amy C. Edmondson, The Fearless Organization: Creating Psychological Safety in the Workplace for Learning, Innovation, and Growth, 1st edition (Hoboken, New Jersey: Wiley, 2018).

[22]Simon Sinek, Why Good Leaders Make You Feel Safe, https://www.ted.com/talks/simon_sinek_why_good_leaders_make_you_feel_safe.

New approaches to organizational and team development

I am also convinced that organizations need to revisit their approach to team development. Sadly, many do not yet regard the subject as fully legitimate. Leaders too often take a limited view and think that team development mostly involves organizing fun outdoor team-building activities. For sure, these can be an excellent way to (re) connect as a team, and with proper analysis and debriefing they can yield important learnings about team dynamics. But nowadays, organizations **must regard team development as integral to their long-term success** and a strategic driver of their overall health and performance. And this goes way beyond building boats or climbing trees.

Yet I still see way too many leaders using team development as a crisis-management tool. They try to avoid it as much as possible, until their teams face more challenges and issues than they can solve on their own. But waiting until a team becomes dysfunctional before seeking help is an unproductive approach. If an illness is addressed too late, it may no longer be curable.

By contrast, **proactive investment in team development** helps teams to make sense of current changes and reorganizations, resolve conflicts before they escalate, and address deteriorating team dynamics before they become dysfunctional.

[23]George Kohlrieser, Susan Goldsworthy, and Duncan Coombe, Care to Dare: Unleashing Astonishing Potential Through Secure Base Leadership, 2nd ed. (Jossey-Bass, 2012).

The following points summarize my vision of
how organizations should address team development.

TEAM DEVELOPMENT PRINCIPLES

- **Invest proactively** in team development and coaching, and give leaders a specific budget for this purpose.

- Take a **coherent** and **structured approach**.

- Use team coaching **systematically**, and view it as a reliable and reproducible way to develop **high-performing teams**.

- Consider **leadership coaching** as a **strategic asset** and an integral part of achieving high performance and effective teamwork.

- **Support leaders** in their team development efforts. For example, HR and learning and development professionals should provide coherent team development roadmaps and offer in-depth reflections on how to structure team coaching based on specific team needs.

- **Anticipate team development issues and needs** and address them in a **timely manner**, by having HR business partners work alongside line managers and leaders. Where possible, this should be done ahead of every important business transformation.

- Conduct an **intense follow-up** after each team coaching workshop. This is key to ensuring the **practical transfer** and **application of the actions** so that they can **have an impact**.

- **Actively involve teams** throughout the team coaching process, and use their feedback to co-design workshops and focus on the specific needs identified.

Organizations that adhere to these principles and proactively support team development will foster higher levels of engagement, morale, and productivity. At the same time, today's VUCA environment means that **teams themselves are becoming more complex** – and the way we regard them needs to change too.

Understanding teams as complex human ecosystems

In the 1960s, the British theorist and consultant Stafford Beer attempted to model different forms of viable systems. His work[24], together with that of fellow researchers such as Ludwig von Bertalanffy and James G. Miller, helped to establish the foundations of general system theory[25]. These thinkers looked for the common characteristics of various living systems found in nature and society. This work formed the basis of the "systemic" approach that was later applied to many different disciplines, from a microscopic level to a more universal scale.

Systemic principles are applicable to fields including physics, molecular biology, biochemistry, ecology and ecosystems, geography, management, socio-economy, psychotherapy, and theology. And they also apply to team and organizational development[26].

[24]Stafford Beer, Diagnosing the System for Organizations, 1st edition (Chichester: Wiley, 1995).

[25]Ludwig von Bertalanffy, General System Theory: Foundations, Development, Applications, Revised (New York: George Braziller Inc, 2015); James Grier Miller, Living Systems (Niwot, Colo: Univ Pr of Colorado, 1995).

[26]Peter Hawkins and Eve Turner, Systemic Coaching: Delivering Value Beyond the Individual, 1st ed. (Routledge, 2019).

Seen from that perspective, a team is similar to other complex systems such as the Earth's climate, living cells and organisms, the human brain, power grids, transportation and communication systems, social and economic organizations (such as cities), and ultimately the entire universe.

Organizational development researchers have used the systems analogy of the living biological organism to pursue a richer understanding of how organizations work. In 1966, Daniel Katz and Robert Zahn published *The Social Psychology of Organizations*[27], in which they applied systems theory concepts to organizational life, and other researchers such as Peter Senge and Margaret J. Wheatley later took a similar approach[28]. This contrasted with the traditional view of organizations as machines that leaders could command and control to increase productivity.

Complex systems are intrinsically difficult to model because of the dependencies, competition, relationships, and other types of interaction between their parts, or between a given system and its environment. Several internal and external factors are constantly at work. These relationships give rise to certain distinct properties such as non-linearity, emergence, spontaneous order, adaptation, and feedback loops, which make such systems too complex to be controlled. That explains why the old command-and-control management system is not suited to managing teams in a VUCA environment.

As in natural ecosystems, a dynamic equilibrium develops over time between the individual components of a team. And as with living organisms at a cellular level, team and context mutually influence each other through an imaginary semi-permeable boundary between them.

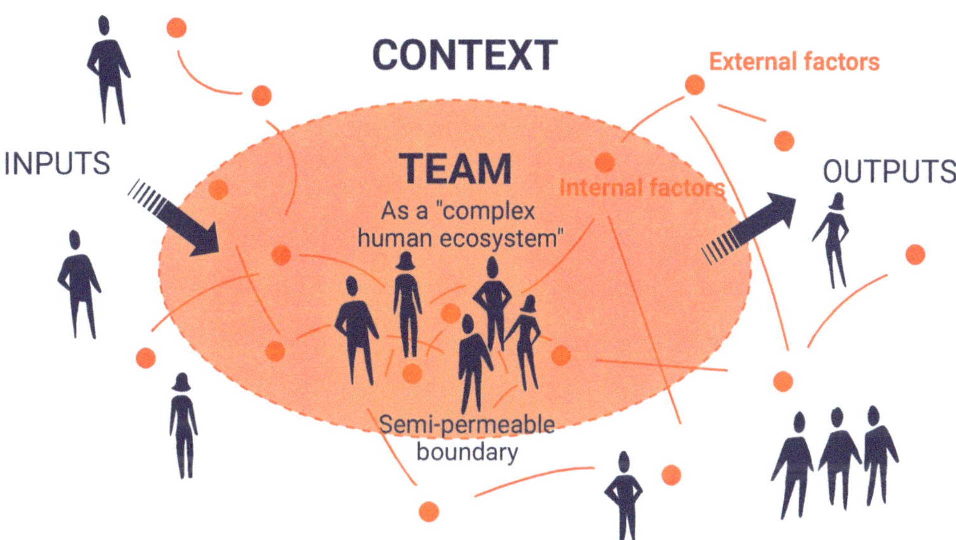

Organizational systems have three main parts: **inputs**, **throughputs**, and **outputs**. It helps to think of such a system as a network in which the nodes represent the individual components and their interactions.

So, I created a model of teams as complex human ecosystems that interact with their environment or context, as shown above:

This results in an open system where the team, the context, and all their constituent parts are interrelated and interdependent. Changes to one sub-part of the system will directly or indirectly influence the others. For example, if a team leader calls in sick, the team will have to adapt and cope with the temporary loss.

[27]Daniel Katz, The Social Psychology of Organizations, 2nd edition (Wiley, 1978).

[28]Margaret J. Wheatley, Leadership and the New Science: Discovering Order in a Chaotic World, 3rd edition (San Francisco: Berrett-Koehler Publishers Inc., 2006).

When things are in balance, some form of homeostasis can take place. The team can operate at its full potential, steadily processing inputs (what is asked of the team) and transforming them into outputs (products, services, and solutions) in order to create value for its stakeholders, including customers and other teams. Sustaining that steady state and maintaining team effectiveness requires attention and **maintenance energy**. If you suddenly decided to stop showering and brushing your teeth, it would not take long until your friends noticed. Likewise, keeping teams healthy and well-functioning requires effort and proactivity from all involved.

As they pursue their goals, teams also need to think carefully about how they create value across their whole ecosystem. Holism, or thinking as a whole, implies that teams should avoid short-term tactics or local actions that have a negative impact in the long run or on other parts of the system. Holistically minded teams should not destroy value at one end of the process in order to create value at the other. Instead, they should establish **integrated value chains** that benefit all stakeholders involved in the wider ecosystem – including the team members themselves, of course.

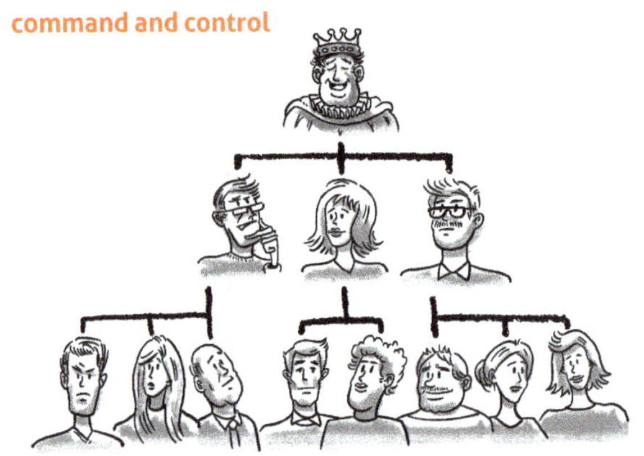

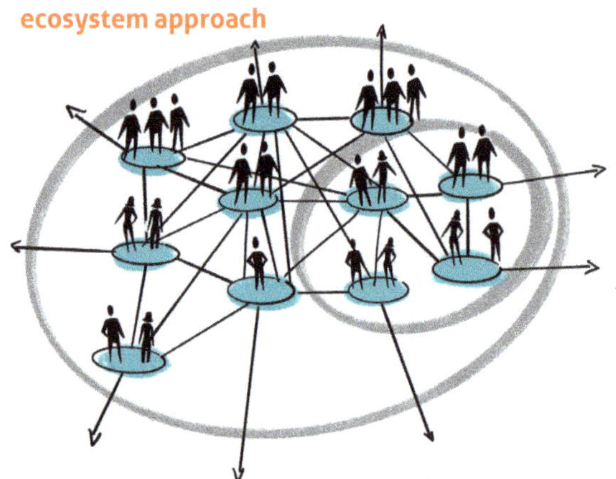

While teams are pursuing their goals, they must remain agile and ready to adapt because the environment may change. Because the environment is by definition unpredictable, teams cannot predetermine the best way to achieve their goals. In complex systems, this is known as the principle of **equifinality**.

Teams will therefore be better off if they are ready to try different possible options as they work toward their goals. That does not mean teamwork equals total chaos. Teams certainly need structure to navigate their environment, but it should not make them too rigid, because they must remain open and adapt to what is happening in their context.

Three core principles

Understanding teams as complex human ecosystems has many implications. It influences how organizations need to engage with their stakeholders. It shapes how leaders need to act and how teams should operate. And it leads to three guiding principles that lie at the heart of my approach to building sustainable teams.

Core Principle No. 1:
Embrace complexity and vulnerability

When leaders and HR professionals ask me to work with a team, they are usually focused on one central issue or major challenge. An important part of my role during the team coaching process is therefore to address this short-term priority while embracing the full complexity of the team and its ecosystem from a medium to long-term perspective.

Quite often, one of the keys to unlocking such situations is to resist binary thinking and instead take a 360° systemic view of the issues facing the team. As Albert Einstein once said, "we cannot solve our problems with the same level of thinking that created them." In complex systems such as teams, the solutions often lie not in the individual components themselves, but in the **interconnections and interdependencies** between them. Only when a majority – if not all – of the team members understand their internal and external dynamics individually and collectively can they start to connect the dots and make sense of the global picture.

So, I am always mindful during a team coaching intervention to challenge the team to dare themselves into exploring their complexity and vulnerability, while simultaneously being a secure base for them so that the team doesn't get lost or go off track during that exploration. This process creates a shared consciousness – a 360° view – of a team's internal dynamics and a profound understanding of their context. Leaders and teams that successfully develop such a holistic view can collectively act in synergy with their whole ecosystem.

To make sense of constant changes in their environment, sustainable teams need to filter down complexity through a systemic framework that guides their actions consistently over time.

But as we progressively start to see that complex global picture, we also progressively become aware of our vulnerability[29]– within ourselves, our teams, and our organizations, and, more broadly, the vulnerability of our universe and all the ecosystems in it. When we fully grasp complexity and vulnerability, we realize that we cannot be in control of our environment. And this has many implications for leaders, teams, and organizations. For leaders, embracing vulnerability can be as simple as holding regular "ask-me-anything" workshops where they expose themselves to questioning and engage in authentic dialogue with their teams.

[29]Brené Brown, Daring Greatly: How the Courage to Be Vulnerable Transforms the Way We Live, Love, Parent, and Lead (London: Portfolio Penguin, 2012).

Clearly, ten brains are more powerful than one. Teams that systematically use their collective intelligence are more creative (through brainstorming), make smarter and more informed decisions, and are better at investigating and solving problems.

But although highly diverse teams potentially have access to a wider range of intelligence, the reality tends to be quite different. In team coaching sessions, such teams often need help to overcome some of the common traps that prevent them from leveraging their collective intelligence. For example, individuals with strong egos, whether team members or part of the organization's leadership, may block the collective intelligence process by wanting to be proven right rather than listening to other people's great ideas. When our ego gets in the way, we become judgmental and tend to criticize others' suggestions, and fail to engage in co-construction and co-creation. Collective intelligence requires going beyond "idea ownership," and instead thinking in terms of "we" rather than "me."

When I work with a team, I always observe whether its members make space for one another during discussions, and whether the team manages to integrate everyone's inputs in the co-creation process. All teams have their habits and patterns when it comes to the use of space within the group. During your next team meeting, try observing and reflecting on the following:

- Who is more introverted/extroverted?

- Who tends to speak more/less than the others?

- Who usually speaks first/last?

- Whose ideas are not heard by the group?

Collective intelligence requires having everyone on board and combining different ways to stimulate, share, and build on each other's ideas. One useful brainstorming technique during team coaching is to start with a "silent writing" session in which everyone notes down their individual thoughts before taking turns to share them with the group in a structured way. Only then does the team start to elaborate on those ideas and select and prioritize the ones to take forward.

To lead sustainable teams successfully, leaders need to develop some kind of inner stability and wisdom that will empower them to use their **freedom of choice** to make pragmatic, consistent, and informed decisions before taking action.

Our freedom of choice is what lies between all the stimuli we get from our environment and our subsequent

On that theme, I can highly recommend the work of Edith Eva Eger, an internationally renowned psychotherapist also known as "the ballerina of Auschwitz." In her book *The Choice*[31], Eger describes her experiences in Auschwitz during World War II and shows how to avoid becoming a victim to whatever circumstances we may face during our journey through life. Although today's business leaders don't face such extreme situations, her emphasis on using freedom of choice to make conscious decisions is nonetheless highly relevant.

responses, behaviors, and actions. In that space, we have the power to choose our response. If we feel that we have no choice, and that we have been taken "hostage" by a certain person or situation, or even sometimes unconsciously by ourselves[30], this is a clear signal that we may have lost that power. We then lose our ability to lead consciously, and feel trapped in dysfunction without knowing how to break free.

One of my goals when coaching leaders is to empower them to promote conscious leadership in themselves and the people they lead. Conscious leadership implies being aware of the social, economic, and ecological impact of our decisions and actions, and of their long-term effect across different systems.

These core principles are part of the fabric from which sustainable teams are made, and form part of their DNA. One key differentiator that sets sustainable teams apart from other teams is their ability to remain true to those guiding principles despite changes in their context.

---

[30]George Kohlrieser, Hostage at the Table: How Leaders Can Overcome Conflict, Influence Others, and Raise Performance, 1st ed. (Jossey-Bass, 2007).

[31]Dr. Edith Eva Eger, The Choice: Embrace the Possible (New York: Scribner, 2017).

KEY LEARNINGS

Part II

1. In our increasingly **VUCA** world, a linear approach to team building and change management does not work anymore. Instead, we need to embrace concepts such as **circularity**, **sustainability**, and **inter-dependability**, and take a more **systemic** view of our interactions with other human beings and our wider environment.

2. Organizations need to reinvent themselves as traditional command-and-control management approaches involving vertical, hierarchical structures make way for more **circular**, **sociocratic** governance systems and **flatter structures**.

3. To navigate in a VUCA context, leaders need to develop **new actitudes**, **empower teams**, and instill a more **participative culture** into their organizations.

4. Nowadays, **team development** has become integral to an organization's **long-term success**, and a strategic driver of its **overall performance and health**.

5. Developing sustainable teams requires seeing them as **complex human ecosystems**. This implies that leaders and teams should embrace **complexity and vulnerability**, leverage **collective intelligence**, and promote **conscious leadership** in themselves and others.

Capture your own

INSIGHTS

....

ACTIONS

....

THINGS TO SHARE

....

PART III – Building Sustainable Teams: An Integrated Framework and Impact Model

The main objective of Part III is to translate the high-level concepts from Part II into an integrated set of tools that are applicable to team development.

This section introduces the 18 Team Sustainability Drivers and argues that focusing on these can yield positive long-run outcomes in terms of team sustainability, business success, customer satisfaction, and ecosystem growth.

Enable, engage, energize

The three core principles that I outlined in Part II are essential to build successful sustainable teams. Developing teams and organizations is a marathon, not a sprint. It involves numerous small choices, behaviors, and actions that at the time don't feel significant. But when completed consistently, these steps have the power to make a dramatic difference over time.

Sustainable teams follow the same logic and principles that Darren Hardy outlines in his book *The Compound Effect*[32]. And his formula captures what leaders should do to develop high-performing sustainable teams:

Small-Smart Choices + Consistency + Time = RADICAL DIFFERENCE over time

This formula makes a lot of sense. But the big challenge for teams and leaders is how to make those smart choices consistently over time given the VUCA context and the turbulence that they must constantly navigate.

Because team development is a long-term process, it is difficult for leaders to know where to focus their efforts. Results take time to measure, and achieving the desired outcomes – such as transforming a team's entire dynamics – usually requires a multifactorial approach.

When I was planning my move into coaching, I spoke with many leaders who were unsure what to do to change their team's dynamics. Those conversations made me realize that having a dedicated framework for developing sustainable teams would help leaders to structure their approach and reduce the risk of doing the wrong thing with their teams.

So, I focused my research on identifying the underlying factors that could help teams to create positive momentum and progressively transform themselves into sustainable teams over time.

---

[32]Darren Hardy, The Compound Effect (Vanguard Press, 2012).

I concluded that such teams successfully manage to get all their members sustainably **enabled**, **engaged**, and **energized** in their work. Achieving this requires sound management of **18 team sustainability drivers** – the building blocks upon which sustainable teams are built over time.

The figure below shows how sustainable teams make those three dimensions work together to achieve and sustain lasting value, organizational health, and superior performance. First, leaders make sure that everyone in the team is fully *enabled* to deliver on his or her mission by having access to the resources, skills, training, and support they need to do the job at hand. Then, they make sure the whole team is mobilized and *engaged*, and understands how their work creates value for customers and other stakeholders. Finally, they build a performance culture that integrates the notion of recovery so that everyone remains *energized* in the long run.

Sustainable teams develop specific habits that enable them to *proactively* manage those three dimensions. For example, they maintain a constant ongoing dialogue and are always aware of their "state." Managing emotional, physical, cognitive, and spiritual states is as important for teams as it is for individuals. This takes a lot of maturity and requires the team to find ways to regulate the whole team's ecosystem across the different circles of influence[33] within an organization, including individuals, teams, departments, business units, and the organization itself.

Another key differentiator of sustainable teams, therefore, is their ability to manage their state individually and – most importantly – collectively as they move between the four quadrants in the diagram below.

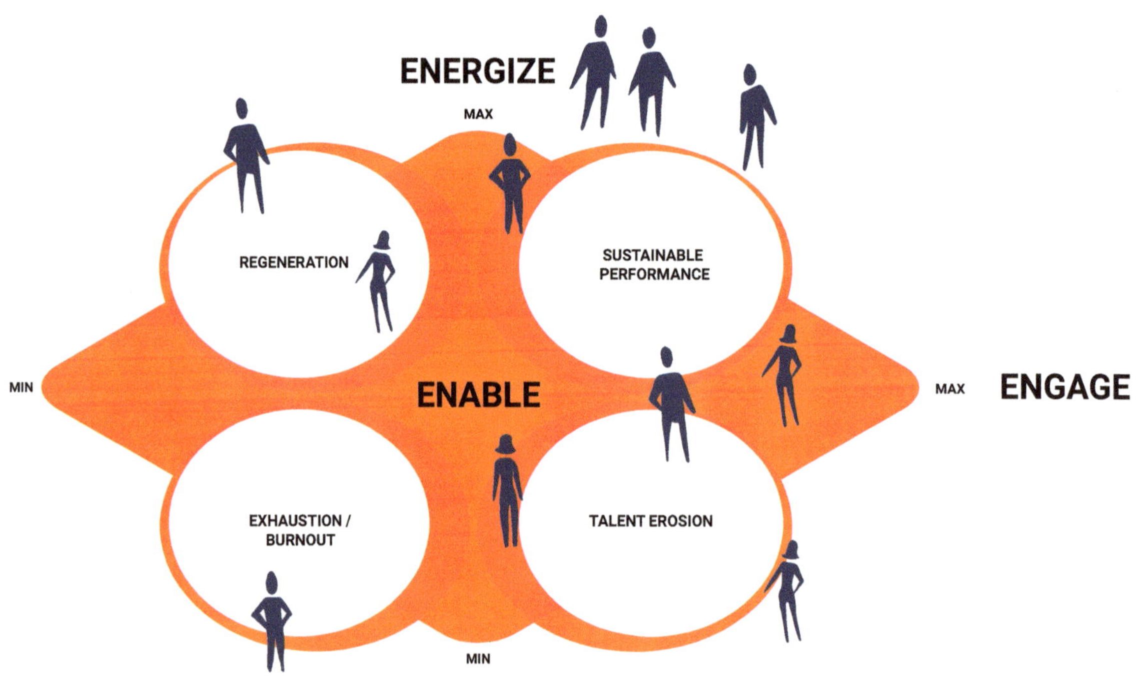

---

[33]Stephen R. Covey, The 7 Habits of Highly Effective People: Powerful Lessons in Personal Change (Mango, 2016).

- **Sustainable performance.** This is the ideal state, but also the most difficult to achieve and maintain. Team members in this quadrant feel that they are fully **enabled**, **engaged**, and **energized**. Sustainable teams are able to grow and keep a majority of their members in this zone over time. That requires maintaining a subtle and dynamic equilibrium between many interdependent factors – namely, the 18 team sustainability drivers, which I will introduce shortly.

- **Talent erosion.** Team members most often move into this quadrant as a result of over-engagement. They are still **enabled** and (over-)**engaged** in their work, but because they are unable to renew their energy sufficiently, they progressively drift into the talent erosion zone. Like natural erosion, the process is slow and gradual and can sometimes be difficult to detect. Denial, whether on the part of the team or the individual, is also an aggravating risk factor in this case. When such a situation is acknowledged, leaders should find ways to reduce the team member's workload temporarily (lower on **engage**) so that he or she can focus on restoring their energy level (higher on **energize**). The person would then hopefully move into the "regeneration" quadrant.

- **Regeneration.** Some leaders and teams may regard this as the most counter-intuitive quadrant, especially in Western cultures that value activity more than rest. But it is the most essential for achieving a sustainable level of engagement and performance. In my experience, this quadrant is also the least socially accepted of the four, because we tend to value results and performance and fail to recognize that recovery and regeneration are an integral part of success. In sports, any athlete who fails to build enough recovery time into their daily, weekly, monthly, and annual training routines would hit the wall prematurely and be forced to stop owing to an injured and exhausted body. Likewise, some of the small-smart choices that can make a radical difference for teams when repeated consistently over time relate to the **energize** dimension. Sustainable teams are able to create a culture that fully integrates and values recovery as part of their definition of performance.

- **Exhaustion/burnout.** This is obviously a quadrant to avoid. When a team member reaches a state of exhaustion and burnout, it not only affects them at many levels but also creates a cascading domino effect in the team. Burnout is usually the result of multiple interdependent factors, with responsibility shared between the individual, the team, their leaders, and the organization. It is often an indication that the team has not yet developed the culture, routine, and habits that it needs to become sustainable.

Someone experiencing exhaustion and burnout needs to disengage and disconnect from their work environment for a while. Their primary focus should be to create a protective zone where they can find the time, space, and support they need to remobilize and replenish their energy. Once they have successfully recovered, they will become progressively ready to re-**engage** into new projects and will feel **enabled** and **energized** to do so.

Different scenarios are possible at this stage. If the burnout was primarily due to overload but the person likes their job and the team offers a supportive environment, then they can usually go back into the same team with an adjusted workload. When the person still perceives the team and/or the organization's leadership as a risk factor, it is usually better for them to move to a more caring environment in another team or organization. Finally, as I know from personal experience, exhaustion can also result from a deeper conflict between an individual's values and their role or profession. In this case, the burnout/exhaustion episode can be an invitation to shift gears and transition into a new career or a role that is more aligned with their values.

When working with teams, I like to use this short list of questions as a check to make sure that we are all on track. These questions are also useful for checking that our collective approach is geared toward the positive outcomes that the team is aiming for in each of the three dimensions.

REALITY CHECK

Enable

● Does the team have access to all the know-how and resources that it needs?

● Is the team fully empowered by the organization? Is it perceived as legitimate, and does it get full support from its leadership, key stakeholders and shareholders?

● Is the team enabled with the right communication tools and platforms so that it can coordinate its activities internally and externally (including with its stakeholders and customers)?

Engage

● What drives collective and individual engagement in the team? Are there any recent examples of a participative approach to decision-making and collective intelligence?

● How does the team and organization define success? Does it include both business and human dimensions? Does it integrate the notion of total value creation? How do team members relate to the team's purpose and mission?

● Do team members have realistic goals that are aligned with the team's roadmap and their individual, team, and organizational vision and mission? Do those goals stimulate teamwork, collaboration, and interdependence across the whole team?

Energize

● Are team members conscious of their "state," and do they manage it proactively through appropriate regulation mechanisms, including team routines, habits, and culture?

● Do the team's leaders and the organization's culture value recovery as part of sustainable performance?

● How does the team channel its energy? Does it nurture energy drivers (stimulating learning, growth, and development), or waste energy in negative patterns such as destructive conflicts and poor use of feedback?

The 18 Team Sustainability Drivers

Having developed this conceptual framework for building sustainable teams, my next challenge was to translate it into practical tools that leaders and teams could use in real life. I wanted these to be easily applicable, but not too simplistic. In particular, I did not want to create another three- or five-step "quick fix" management model. By its very nature, such a framework would have betrayed the notions of complexity and systemicity that are intrinsic to envisioning teams as complex human ecosystems. So, I developed the **18 team sustainability drivers** that you can see below.

All 18 drivers play an important role in helping teams to achieve and sustain high performance – and my vision of team development is that people and business should go hand in hand. So, as you become familiar with the drivers, you will see that they are about striving to fulfill a vision, mission, and goals and caring about team members on a human level. They are also about delivering new products and solutions to the market and creating value for all stakeholders along the value chain.

Developing sustainable teams does not mean growing the business and then taking care of teams, people, and soft skills as a separate matter. Instead, the 18 team sustainability drivers:

● are all **interrelated** and must be managed **simultaneously**, or else there will not be any **synergies**, and

● form an **interdependent**, **holistic system** of **focal points** and a **shared language** across the organization.

We will soon see how the different drivers are interrelated. But let's first look at them individually to see which dimensions of teamwork they cover.

COMMON PURPOSE & VISION

Do we have a clear vision, common purpose, and raison d'être for our team?
Did we express our aspirations and hopes, and how we think this team can have an impact?

SUPPORTIVE LEADERSHIP

Is our team fully legitimate in the eyes of the organization's senior executives?
Are we confident that we can get all the support we need from our leaders,
regardless of the circumstances?

RESOURCES & KNOW-HOW

Do we have the resources and know-how needed to accomplish our mission?
Do we have enough people, time, budget, equipment, skills, and experience?

CUSTOMER EXPERIENCE

Did we define our target customers and stakeholders both inside and outside the organization?
What steps can we take to continuously enhance our customers' overall experience?

DEPENDABILITY & TEAMWORK

Do we genuinely want to form a team and engage in teamwork?
Are we confident enough to rely and depend on each other?

LEARNING, GROWTH, PROGRESS

Does our environment stimulate learning, growth, and progress?
Do we capture the opportunities to learn from one another in this team?

ENTHUSIASM & POSITIVE ATTITUDE TOWARD CHANGE

Are we open to change?
Do we maintain a positive attitude and see opportunities through change?

INSPIRING GOALS: SELF & TEAM

Do we set, and believe in, inspiring goals that foster collaboration within our team?
Are we individually and collectively mobilized to achieve them?

COMMUNICATION TOOLS & PLATFORMS

Are we empowered with the right tools and platforms to communicate
and collaborate swiftly in the digital era?
Are the formats and frequency of our meetings adequate, useful, and productive?

STAKEHOLDER & RISK MANAGEMENT

Do we engage effectively with our stakeholders?
Do we proactively identify potential threats that could impact our team, and manage risks?

CLEAR ROLES & PROCESSES

Are we clear on everyone's roles and responsibilities in the team?
Do we have clear processes and workflows, especially for decision-making?

WORKPLACE DESIGN & ERGONOMICS

Does our workplace energize us to engage in effective collaboration?
Is the use of space modular? Are there areas for collaboration
as well as spaces to focus, rest, and recover?

WORK-LIFE & ENERGY MANAGEMENT

Is work-life balance and energy management part of our team culture?
Are individual needs discussed within the team?

RECOGNITION & REWARD

Is our team's performance appropriately acknowledged and rewarded?
Do we give and receive regular positive reinforcement within the team?

INNOVATION & VALUE CREATION

Does our environment and organizational culture foster innovation and sustainable value creation? Are we empowered to take risks, try new things, and explore new ways to develop and deliver our solutions?

STRATEGY, ROADMAP, & PRIORITIES

Do we regularly review the adequacy of our team's strategy, roadmap, and priorities given the latest changes in our context?
Do we use a visual team roadmap? Are we all aligned on the same priorities?

PSYCHOLOGICAL SAFETY & TRUST

Do we feel secure enough to explore vulnerabilities within the team?
Do we invest time and effort to build trust, connect with each other, and establish deeper relationships within the team?

CONFLICT & FEEDBACK MANAGEMENT

Are we able to deal with disagreement constructively and come out with better solutions?
Do we use conflicts as opportunities to know each other better through genuine feedback and authentic dialogues filled with empathy and compassion?

In Part IV, I present three real-world case studies of team coaching interventions where teams used the 18 drivers to address their respective challenges. And in Part V, I summarize the dos and don'ts for each driver to help guide leaders and teams as they implement them. This will help your team to avoid common pitfalls and rapidly implement successful practices related to the drivers.

The 18 team sustainability drivers should never be considered in isolation from each other, because they form an ecosystem in themselves. That is why my colleagues and I like to use a circular map of the drivers during our team coaching interventions.

This circular model is an extremely useful reminder that team challenges are more complex than they seem. Thoughtful decisions require leaders to consider the inter relationships between the 18 drivers, because these are vital to the healthy long-run functioning of a team. This approach helps teams to tackle their current challenges while keeping an eye on the wider context and other dimensions involved in upcoming team transformations.

The same logic applies to how organizations should manage the 18 drivers. Leading teams in a turbulent VUCA context involves constantly zooming in and out to focus more on the specific topics requiring attention now, without losing sight of the bigger picture. And that is exactly where I see many teams and leaders struggling.

When teams and leaders are under pressure, they often narrow their focus to a single dimension – their number one top priority now – but at the cost of totally neglecting everything else. The organization becomes monomaniacal. The hot topic becomes the new buzzword on everyone's lips, and people lose their peripheral vision as it becomes their only focal point. But although such a focus may be useful in the short term, leaders and teams should not ignore the other peripheral dimensions for too long.

A juggling analogy helps to illustrate the underlying dynamics between the 18 drivers. If you are juggling with balls, you need to focus more on catching the ones approaching your hands while simultaneously keeping the others that are still in the air in your peripheral vision. You anticipate that you will soon need to shift focus to grab these following balls and propel them in the air. To keep all the balls moving, you can't afford to focus on only one, because pretty soon all the others will hit the floor.

Unfortunately, too many organizations make exactly this mistake, and usually learn the hard way that neglecting important aspects of teamwork has a cost. After some time, they experience a boomerang effect, as dimensions that have been neglected for too long hit back. But people are not even aware that the boomerang is flying in their direction, because they are 100% focused on their top priority and have lost their peripheral vision.

So, when the boomerang hits them painfully at full speed, it becomes their new focal point, a burning issue they must resolve with the utmost urgency. This is what I call the "reductionism trap."

Don't get me wrong: it is important to set priorities. Especially when the organizational ship needs steering through a turbulent period, leadership clearly involves choosing the right battles and focusing efforts on what will have the most impact. But conscious leaders can do that while simultaneously keeping sight of the wider systemic context in which teams operate. They are able to operate on one organ while maintaining the others and hence keeping the whole body in a functional state. That is what conscious leadership is all about: being able to ponder the cost of actions and inaction in all areas that are ultimately vital to the organization.

An integrated framework and impact model

Nowadays, many people are ringing the alarm bell and raising red flags about the way our economies work. In particular, our long-standing inappropriate use of re-sources is unbalancing many ecosystems and ultimately putting humans and other species at risk. But for some reason, we fail to acknowledge the need for change, and consequently do not take the appropriate actions. Our habits are deeply ingrained, and we are often unaware of the underlying dynamics that could help us to modify our routines[34]. It is hard enough to change our habits in response to things affecting us today, and even harder when we perceive the threats as being more distant.

The same dynamic is at play within organizations. We live in a fast-paced society that demands instant gratification and expects any challenges to be resolved immediately. Because the vast majority of organizations are geared toward delivering short-term results, they tend to focus on initiatives from which they expect rapid returns. The key to successfully building sustainable teams, therefore, is to ensure that short-term actions will not negatively impact the whole team ecosystem in the long term.

My integrated framework and impact model on the facing page shows how focusing on the 18 team sustainability drivers can yield positive long-run outcomes in terms of team sustainability, business success, customer and stake-holder satisfaction, and ecosystem growth. The model incorporates two fundamental laws that I applied to team and organizational development: the law of cause and effect, and the fact that results take time to measure.

[34]Charles Duhigg, The Power of Habit: Why We Do What We Do, and How to Change (William Heinemann Ltd, 2012).

FRAMEWORK & IMPACT MODEL

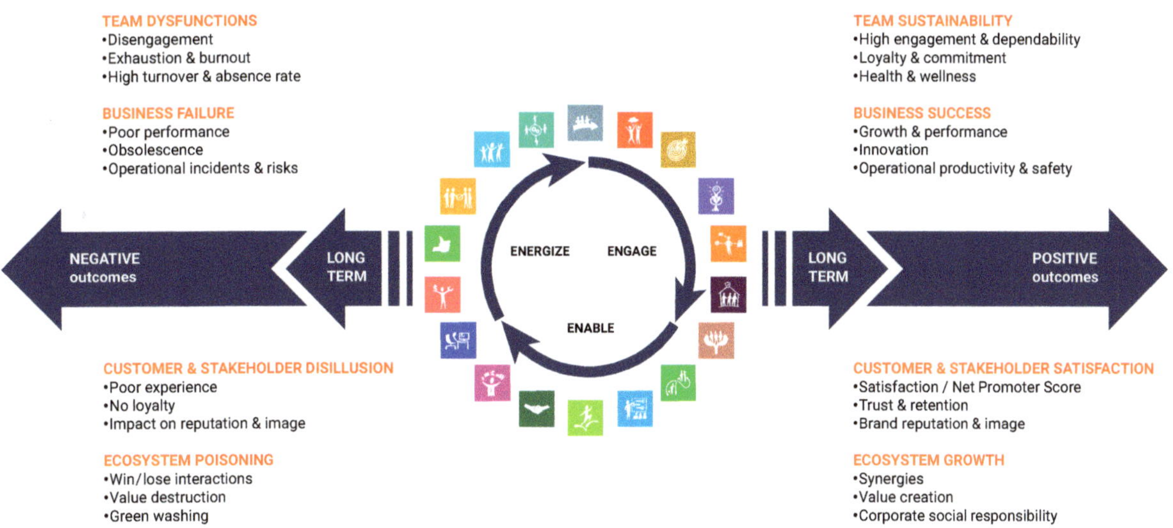

Teams and their leaders must constantly adapt to new challenges in their environment, and the choices they make today will have compounding effects that produce either a negative or positive long-run impact. That is why it is so important to promote a culture of conscious leadership across the whole organization. Sustainable teams need to make conscious choices every day. So, organizations must ensure that leaders and teams – even when under pressure – are constantly aware of the bigger picture, and are accountable for, conscious of, and connected with the cumulative effects of their actions.

Because sustainable teams' outcomes are the cumulative result of moment-to-moment choices, teams have incredible power to change their outcomes by changing their decisions. Step by step and day by day, their choices will shape their actions until they become habits that are part of the team's routines.

Although there often is no direct cause-effect relationship, the decisions that a team takes or avoids now will drive organizational health and performance in the long run. And as the case studies in Part IV will show, the integrated framework and impact model aims to help teams make the right choices today.

KEY LEARNINGS

Part III

1. Building sustainable teams involves a number of **small choices**, **behaviors**, and **actions** that at the time don't feel significant. But when completed consistently, these steps have the power to **make a radical difference over time**.

2. Sustainable teams successfully manage to get all their members sustainably **enabled**, **engaged**, and **energized** in their work.

3. The **18 team sustainability drivers** are all **interrelated** and must be **managed simultaneously**, and form an **interdependent**, **holistic system** of focal points and a **shared language** across the organization.

4. Leading teams in a turbulent VUCA context is **like juggling** and requires maintaining a focus on the specific topics needing attention now, while not losing sight of the bigger picture.

Capture your own

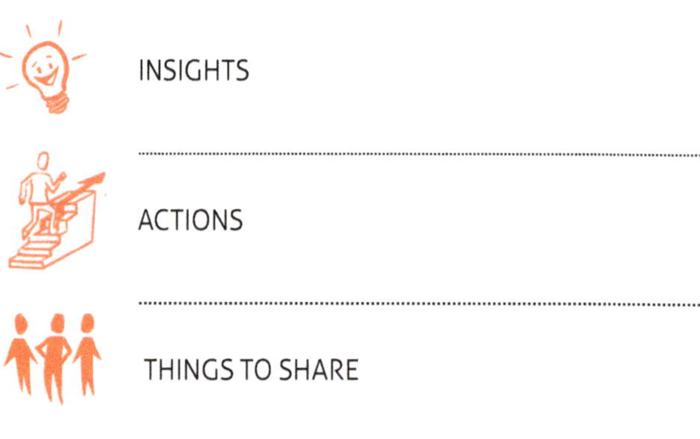

INSIGHTS

....

ACTIONS

....

THINGS TO SHARE

....

PART IV – Building Sustainable Teams: From Idea to Practice

The main objective of Part IV is to show you how you can make practical use of the 18 team sustainability drivers to coach teams in real life.

This section takes you through three real-world case studies where my colleagues and I applied the sustainable teams approach in coaching interventions, and discusses the challenges that we faced while working with those teams.

It all starts with the foundations

Building sustainable teams is like building a house. It all begins with the foundations, and these are provided by senior executives. When a member of the leadership team cuts the ribbon on a project, or takes the first step in a new initiative, their actions symbolize commitment. And the same applies to building sustainable teams.

Although miracles do occasionally happen, sustainable teams generally emerge only when organizations truly support and apply the underlying concepts that I covered in Part II (the three core principles) and Part III (the 18 team sustainability drivers together with the integrated framework and impact model). Executives and board members must fully adopt and consistently display the mindsets, behaviors, and habits that are aligned with those core principles. Only then can the organization's culture diffuse a sense of what leadership, collaboration, and teamwork really mean. And if leaders and teams consistently make smart conscious choices over time, positive effects will compound and start to show results – and sustainable teams will begin to emerge across the organization.

So, when an organization wants to start a new team coaching initiative, it needs to conduct a reality check in several areas. I've listed the most important of these on the following page.

REALITY CHECK

Governance/board

Does your organization's governance promote sustainable results and sustainable teams? Or is it more focused on short-term results, giving little consideration to compounded longer-term outcomes?

CEO

Does your board strongly support and empower your CEO? Can she promote sustainable teams across the organization? Or is she under so much pressure that she instead cascades down an overwhelming amount of steam that does more harm than good to the teams?

Leadership team

Do your board and executive leadership team function as sustainable teams themselves? Or is there an obvious lack of teamwork due to excessive egos, interpersonal conflicts, or a lack of mutual support or accountability, for example?

Cross-functional project teams

Does your organization truly empower cross-functional teams? Or do they regularly face resistance due to the conflicting demands and interests of departments that would prefer to operate as hermetic silos?

Functional teams/departments

Does your unit truly engage in teamwork? Is it a high-performing sustainable team?

Stakeholders/customers

Does your organization engage sustainably with its stakeholders? Does it seek to create value for all stakeholders along the value chain, including suppliers, employees, and the wider community? Or does it seek to maximize its profits without much consideration for the other players?

Ecosystem

Is your organization conscious of its interdependence and interactions with its context/environment, and the resulting impacts (both positive and negative)? Or does it operate without much care for the wider ecosystem?

I realize that emphasizing the role of executives and board members seems like a rather hierarchical and top-down approach, but the same questions hold true for more holistic and circular organizational models. Whatever the model, organizations and their leaders must create the right context for sustainable teams to emerge.

Before embarking on any intervention, therefore, I always check first whether my colleagues and I have the right context to operate by scanning through the questions listed above. Potential gaps or problems must be identified and discussed as early as possible in the team coaching or organizational development process, so that coaches don't end up swimming against the tide. Building sustainable teams is never simple, but the process is much easier when coaching interventions are supported by the right organizational dynamics.

Prepare, prepare, prepare

Preparation is another critical success factor when building sustainable teams. It should include an in-depth briefing among all key stakeholders – HR professionals, leaders, and coaches – involved in designing and delivering the team development program. The brief should focus on understanding the team's background, current dynamics, and business goals, and adapting the intervention's content and format to help it face upcoming challenges with confidence.

The preparation phase is key to understanding the explicit and implicit reasons that drive leaders and HR departments to initiate team development. Here are some of the most frequent ones:

TEAM TROUBLES

Severe cases

The team is at risk and under strong pressure from its main stakeholders. This may be the result of the team's negative image and reputation, recurrent customer dissatisfaction, chronic team underperformance, high costs compared to the value created, or redundancies following mergers or internal reorganizations.

Common problems include:

● **Destructive interpersonal conflicts** resulting in a dislocated team, loss of empathy, and sometimes violent communication and behaviors.

● **Dysfunctional, toxic, and manipulative behaviors** within the team or by their leaders.

● **Covert (sometimes overt) sabotage**, often linked to past decisions that continue to fuel strong resistance and disagreement within the team.

● **High levels of turnover, sick leave, and burnout**, often caused by strong external pressure on a team that lacks resources and know-how, or access to a network that it can leverage.

● **Broken bonds and polarized subgroups**, reflecting a deep lack of trust between team members and/or their leaders stemming from unresolved past events and circumstances.

● **Team trauma** resulting from successive transformations and disruptions. Team members are locked in fear and anxiety and cannot remobilize their energy toward a common vision for the future. The team gets insufficient support and perhaps cannot trust its leaders to help it move forward from the current situation.

Milder situations

Team members demonstrate a lack of commitment and buy-in, function more as a workgroup than a real team, and are not truly mobilized around a common purpose, vision, and mission.

Common problems include:

● **Poor decision-making processes**, resulting in lack of team involvement and participation in key decisions.

● **Lack of cohesion, mutual help, and support**. Team members work mostly as individual contributors rather than interdependently on common projects.

● **Lack of clarity on the team's roadmap and priorities**. Team members are not aligned, and do not really cooperate to find synergies or work interdependently to achieve common goals.

● **Operationally inefficient teamwork**. Team members are frustrated by inefficient processes and by a lack of clarity regarding their respective roles and responsibilities.

● **Poor communication**, resulting from organizational silos and a lack of trust among team members from different units. This is often linked to tensions and loyalty conflicts in a matrix organization.

● **The illusion of perpetual harmony**. Hyper-cohesive teams may avoid conflict and repress any form of disagreement among their members, thus blocking new ideas, collective intelligence, and creativity.

During the preparation phase, I always challenge myself to adapt and customize the development program to each team. This is key, for three reasons. First, team development does not follow a one-size-fits-all approach. Second, I want to avoid being too dogmatic and rigid about the use of a predefined methodology that does not fully match the team's needs. And third, imposing a standardized model runs contrary to my philosophy of leveraging collective intelligence through a participative co-development approach.

The preparation and adaptation phase also brings everyone onto the same page, and allows space and time to deal with any "elephant in the room" topics that need to be addressed ahead of the project.

When going live, be ready to meet resistance

For many organizations, building sustainable teams implies a paradigm shift. It requires major changes in the way organizations and their leaders deal with:

- short-term vs. long-term goals

- control vs. vulnerability/complexity

- profit maximization vs. value co-creation

- top-down management vs. participative decision-making based on collective intelligence.

Like any other change, this will induce resistance at different levels within an organization.

One type of resistance is evident at **board and executive level.** In organizations where leadership teams are under constant pressure to deliver, people do not dare to change their approach to team and organizational development because they fear this will negatively impact performance. And falling short of investors' expectations could have implications for their bonus and career prospects.

But what board members and senior executives fail to acknowledge is that their organizations are hostages to the limitations of their current status quo. Change will not be possible until a critical mass of leaders dares to embrace it and adopt the new sustainable teams paradigm. Even if the adaptation and learning phase results in a moderate short-term dip in performance, leaders should frame this not as a loss, but as an investment that will yield higher levels of sustainable performance as the organization leverages the power of sustainable teams over time.

Again, performance here does not simply mean financial performance. As I mentioned already, I define the term more broadly to include dimensions related to team sustainability, business success, customer and stakeholder satisfaction, and ecosystem growth.

Another frequent barrier are the **teams themselves**, including their **leaders**. Every team, at one level or another, will likely initially resist any form of team development effort. Although they often don't express their resistance overtly, skepticism and frustrations resulting from previous team-building exercises can potentially be a powerful obstacle to fresh coaching interventions, as I discovered during the following recent client project.

Working with Justin and his team

This coaching intervention with Justin's team was part of a global transformation project that included several teams within their organization.

Before initiating workshops with individual teams, my colleagues and I had carefully planned and prepared this project with the organization's board and leadership team.

I thought we had done it all by the book. I thought all team leaders had understood our approach to building sustainable teams, and were fully on board and receptive. Justin himself had actively participated in the project kick-off with the other team leaders, and had helped to put together:

- a detailed project roadmap outlining each project phase and its goals, activities, and expected outcomes. This was presented and approved by the board and leadership team (including Justin).

- a pilot version of the workshop with the leadership team (including Justin). We then integrated the leadership team's feedback on the workshop's format and content before deploying it across individual teams.

- an all-hands kick-off conference to communicate the project before conducting workshops with the teams.

But I nearly fell out of my chair when Justin started his introductory speech at the beginning of our first workshop with his team. "Before we start the day," he said, "I must say that some of us are skeptical about such workshops. We have already done this two years ago. We worked with a consultant who had us play games and climb into trees. That was fun, but we did not get anything out of the exercise. It had no impact on us as a team and did not help us in any way. We are quite busy now, and I am not sure this time is well invested."

When I heard this, I initially felt furious. I interpreted Justin's initial statement as a form of sabotage, and a betrayal of the trust we had built with the leaders in the early phase of the project.

Internally, I was thinking, "What do you mean, climbing into trees? Our workshops have been co-developed with your leadership team to bring a structured approach to leveraging your team's collective intelligence. We've agreed with your leadership team to collect all the ideas developed by the teams, and to follow up and commit by taking tangible actions in order to have an impact at individual, team, and organizational level."

But I also knew that being defensive or passive-aggressive would not help. To move forward, I had to empathize with what Justin had expressed. To do that, I first had to deal with my own emotions, let go of my ego's defense mechanisms, restore an internal feeling of safety, and shift my mind's eye toward resolving the situation positively.

So, I took a deep breath before I replied. "I fully share your worries about the effectiveness of such team workshops," I began. "I hear that some of you are skeptical and doubtful, and I thank you for being honest and expressing this upfront. In fact, one of my main worries when I work with teams is that our workshops will only be ephemeral events and will have no real impact on the team in the long run. That is the reason why we have designed this workshop in two phases." (I then went on to explain the workshop design and expected outcomes.)

"And the only way for us to ensure this will have an impact is to make a contract with your team. I need to be sure that despite your initial skepticism, you are ready to give it a chance. I need to hear that you are on board and ready to engage in the process. I need to trust that you will follow up and hold each other accountable for your commitments, both individually and collectively as a team.

"So, does this work for you?" I asked. "Are you willing to give it a try?"

And to my surprise, the team members started looking at each other and nodding their heads. Some of them were even smiling, and I thought I saw light and hope in their eyes.

When Justin later concluded the session, the mood was very different to the one at the start. "I have to say that although I had been critical at the beginning, today was actually extremely helpful," he said. "We have identified a few points that can directly have an impact on us. I will make sure we follow up so that we can rapidly implement this with the team. It was great to take this time with the team and I believe we should actually do it more often!"

This experience, although painful, taught me a lot about how to handle teams' resistance.

I realized that in most – if not all – group coaching interventions, it is natural for teams to be somewhat skeptical at the beginning of a team development program. While some team members may be looking forward to the exercise, others may be more doubtful, and have their own reasons for being cautious or critical.

Part of my role as a facilitator is to welcome those doubts (instead of discarding them), invite team members to express them, and dig into those resistances until we understand their root causes. Encouraging a team to air its frustrations, explore the underlying emotions, and identify their unmet needs and aspirations is actually a cornerstone of any team development process.

What Justin did was simply to clearly express his own doubts, and, more importantly, to create a safe context for his team members to share their own concerns and skepticism. And he did this right at the start of the team coaching process. Although Justin took me by surprise – it was the first time that a team leader had done a 180-degree switch after having prepared a workshop with me – I am grateful in retrospect for what he did.

His action took courage and was in fact a great way to push us to be authentic and share our doubts and feelings for the rest of the session. When such emotions are left unexpressed, they can undermine the whole team coaching process.

Nowadays, I usually play devil's advocate and acknowledge upfront that teams may be uncomfortable with team development. I tend to do this right after the first round of introductions, and find that it helps to build trust with the group before we can ignite further team development.

Coaching teams through change

"The only constant in life is change." – Heraclitus

Change affects us all every day, and each of us deals with it differently. Likewise, organizations and teams must constantly adapt to both internal and external changes.

We can classify different types of change according to the extent of the change required, the speed with which it is to be achieved, and whether or not it was anticipated[35]. Team coaching can be a powerful tool to help teams cope with and navigate through change.

This is especially true for major changes – either planned and proactive or unforeseen and reactive – that require a paradigm shift and a major revision of a team's modus operandi:

● **Transformations** are often incremental yet fundamental changes that necessitate a change in an organization's culture, because they cannot be handled within the existing organizational paradigm. Team coaching is usually planned and conducted ahead of the upcoming change, as a proactive step to help teams successfully leverage foreseen changes in their context.

● **Disruptions** are sudden major changes that typically force teams and organizations into reactive transformations requiring simultaneous initiatives on many fronts, and often in a relatively short timeframe. In such situations, team coaching is usually triggered reactively to help teams cope with their unforeseen circumstances. Leading and coaching teams through turbulence requires an ability to help them process emotions, re-establish stability and safety, and make critical decisions, while inspiring them to envision a brighter future beyond their current challenges.

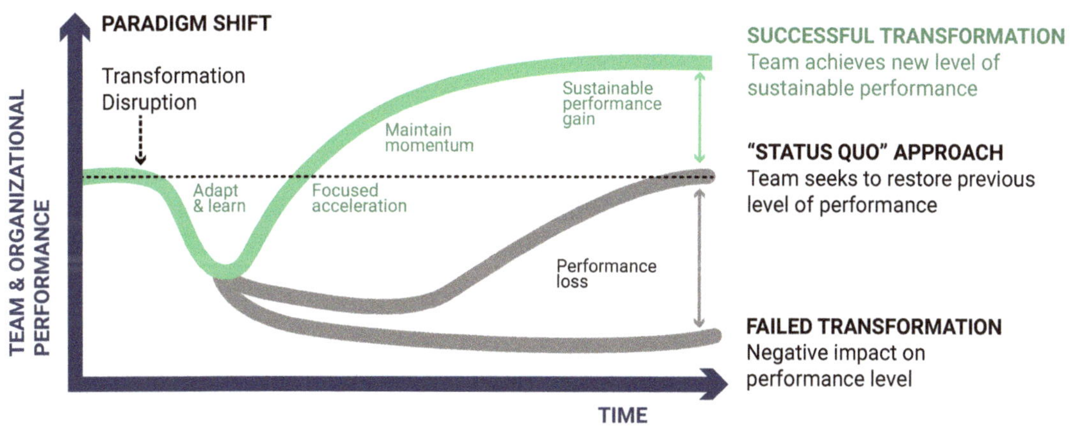

N.B. Performance in this context does not mean only financial performance. I define the term more broadly to include dimensions related to team sustainability, business success, customer/stakeholder satisfaction, and ecosystem growth.

[35]Harvard Business Review et al., HBR's 10 Must Reads on Change Management, 1st edition (Harvard Business Review Press, 2011).

But as the diagram on the previous page shows, the nature and circumstances of a change do not dictate how teams will subsequently perform over time. Regardless of whether a team is facing a transformation or a disruption, what matters is how it handles that change.

How a team embraces a particular change will lead to different outcomes:

Failed transformation

Changes require us to revisit old habits and transform ourselves. Teams may need to reinvent their customer engagement, find new business models, or integrate new technologies. Organizations, meanwhile, may need to invest in emerging markets, create new partnerships, or instigate a culture change, among other things.

Teams and organizations that were already fragile may be unable to cope with a new disruption, because they lack the resilience and resources to invest the energy required by the transformation efforts. This may be due to a combination of factors, including weak financial performance, an exhausted workforce, lack of support from investors, and poor leadership during this and previous disruptions. As a result, the team or organization will fail to embrace major changes and will be negatively impacted in the long run. In the worst cases, their activities will be terminated, and the remaining assets and people relocated to other ventures either inside or outside the organization.

"Status quo" approach

In any transformation, there is a part of the past that we need to let go, and a loss that we need to acknowledge and grieve. Only by going through the grief cycle and processing the emotions (anger, sadness, and fear) associated with each stage of grief can we then reconnect with hope and the joy of life toward the end of the process. "Successful" grief will enable us to integrate the loss into our identity instead of dissociating ourselves from it and freezing the emotions and subparts of ourselves that are linked to the loss. Once our grief is over, we can envision the future with renewed energy and inspiration.

The same is true for teams and organizations. Organizations that fail to grieve their losses do not accept the loss resulting from disruptive change, and will instead try to re-establish what they had before. In their efforts to return to the previous status quo, they will fail to capture the opportunities that are inherent in any transformation, and will merely manage to restore previous performance levels.

Successful transformation

Changes also bring opportunities. To capture them, teams need to be able during grief to look at what they can learn from their loss and consider how they can adapt to their new context. Such teams quickly refine their strategy and remobilize their energy. They consciously decide to focus their efforts on a few targeted accelerations that will help them create a new drive and regain momentum.

The 18 team sustainability drivers are especially useful in this phase. They enable teams to quickly map important changes in their context and choose the right drivers to handle the transition successfully. The compounded effects of sustainable teams' decisions will translate into sustainable performance over time and bring benefits at many levels.

Using collective intelligence in team coaching interventions

My goal in team coaching is to empower teams with the right tools and mindset to successfully embrace such change. Ideally, this should be initiated prior to major transformations. In fact, in our current VUCA context, it should be an integral part of any form of teamwork. Teams that are equipped with such tools will have a competitive advantage and be more resilient in the face of changes in their environment.

Brainstorming sessions and interactive team workshops are common nowadays, and can be powerful ways of

This was a recurrent need in most of our team workshops, and because I could not find appropriate tools to facilitate this type of teamwork, I decided to develop one. My circular **Collective Intelligence Framework** (see diagram below) enables teams to define a common central focus point – one of the 18 team sustainability drivers – and then map the different dimensions or drivers related to this topic in the adjacent Circle 1. Although the framework is similar to the mind-mapping technique, its design also allows for efficient prioritization and decision-making regarding the options that teams develop.

To make my team coaching sessions hands-on and interactive, I make a big circle on the floor using rope, and arrange 18 illustrated cubes around it – one for each sustainable team driver. These cubes are about 30x30x30 centimeters in size. This set-up requires the team to form a physical circle, instead of facing each other or standing

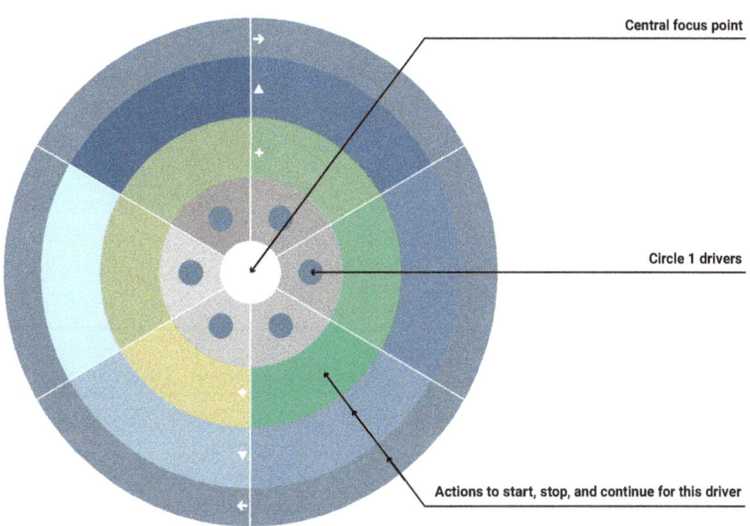

engaging participants in co-creation. But most existing tools take a linear approach to structuring work and information. For example, visual management boards usually use columns and cards to organize tasks and workflows among team members. They are efficient tools for increasing team effectiveness in the operational and implementation phase, but are not optimal for performing other tasks that require a circular, holistic, and systemic approach.

side by side. It also encourages a more collaborative mindset, because everyone can directly see how one another's inputs contribute to their common goal. Team members then debate and vote on which driver should go in the center, and which six should go in Circle 1.

This tool is highly adaptable and versatile, and helps teams to leverage their collective intelligence in a number of situations. When using it with teams, I sometimes

of the session with a shared vision and strong buy-in. And I am always grateful for those moments when collective effort sparks or reactivates the magic of great teamwork.

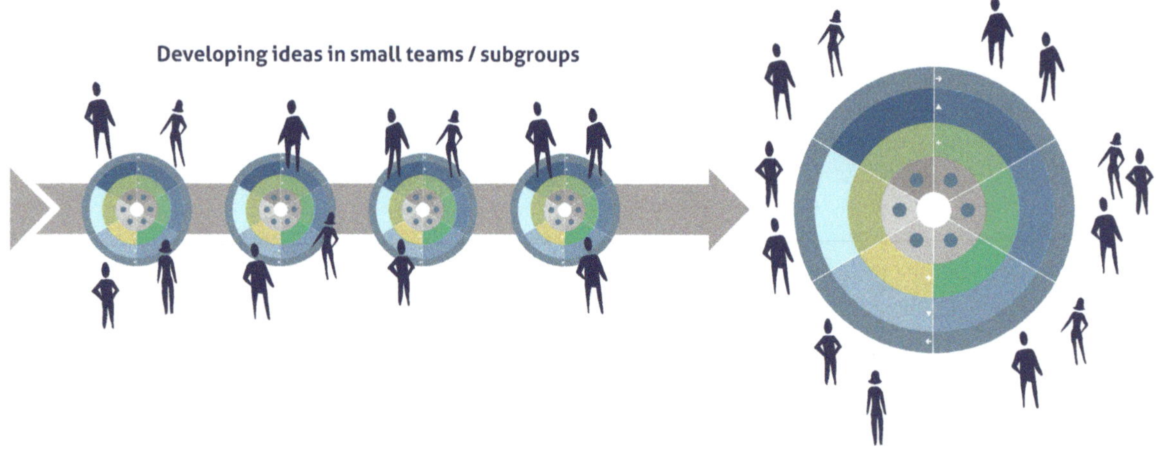

bring more structure to the exercise by defining the central focus point and the six related dimensions in Circle 1. On other occasions, I pose an open question to induce team reflection, and leave it up to the team to decide how they would like to work around the circle.

I am always amazed and positively surprised by the quality and creativity of the insights that teams generate during this process. For some teams, the exercise can induce a complete transformation in the way they collaborate, listen to one another, and collectively develop a systemic understanding of their context. Teams often tell me that they had "serious fun" together and came out

The collective intelligence tool is one of the pillars of my approach to coaching sustainable teams, and incorporates all three of the core principles that I highlighted in Part II. It combines the need to embrace complexity with the need to leverage collective intelligence, and it enables conscious leadership and decision-making.

The following three case studies illustrate how these tools can be applied with teams in real-life situations. Although my colleagues and I don't necessarily follow a linear step-by-step process when working with teams, I present each case study here with a similar workflow across the different project phases, as outlined in the figure below:

Case study No. 1: Transformation of an NGO

In recent years, my colleagues and I have coached three NGOs through major transformations that required significant adjustments of their governance, leadership, and teams. One organization was active at a local and city level, another at national level, and the third had an international scope. Although they had different purposes, all three organizations were facing similar challenges and had to adapt quickly in order to survive important changes in their environment. This case study focuses on the international NGO.

Although the NGO was well established and had a good reputation in its field of expertise, it had been impacted by a paradigm shift in recent years. Some major projects had reached completion and their funding had not been renewed, while several new NGOs had emerged in that area and were competing for the same financial resources.

The situation had progressively snowballed into what the board described as an "unprecedented crisis" for the NGO. The organization had suffered project cuts, reduced its staff by 50%, and faced huge uncertainty about whether it could secure financing for the current and upcoming year.

A few months previously, the board had appointed a new leadership team from which it was expecting a prompt reaction. In particular, the board quickly wanted to see an updated strategy, vision, and roadmap for the coming

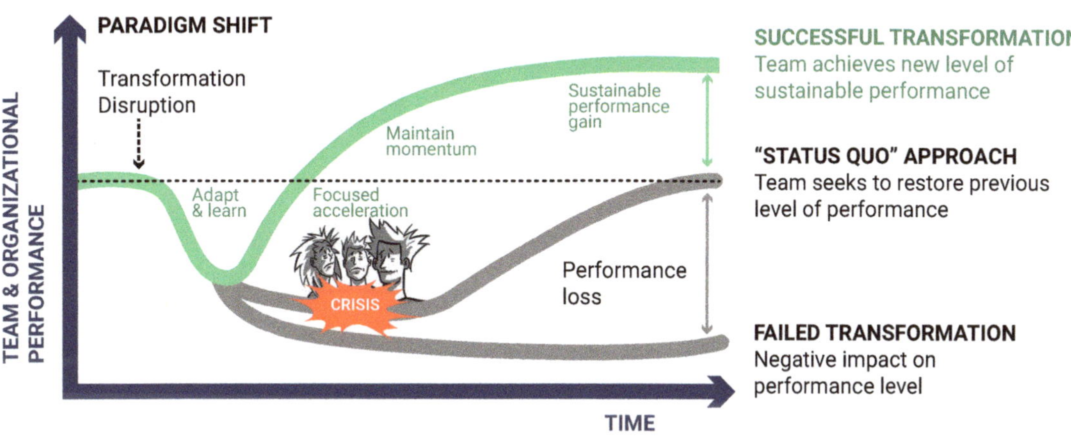

Initial situation/context

The previous 3-5 years had been extremely tough for this NGO, mainly owing to a significant decrease in its income (it was funded primarily through institutional donors and research grants).

3-4 years. This would have to be approved and communicated both internally and externally, including to the NGO's main institutional donors and key country and regional partners.

The board realized that the new leadership team would need support to deal with the crisis, and had therefore allocated a budget for team coaching and organizational development.

Team energy and state

At the start of the project, I quickly realized that the vast majority of the NGO's leadership team and staff were in the Talent Erosion and Exhaustion/Burnout quadrants (see diagram).

found itself stuck in a negative feedback loop that was yielding few results while adding to the workload of an already exhausted group.

On the other hand, I noticed during the first workshop that a few team members were clearly disengaged. When I asked them how they related to the current situation, they said that they felt powerless and needed to protect themselves from exhaustion and burnout.

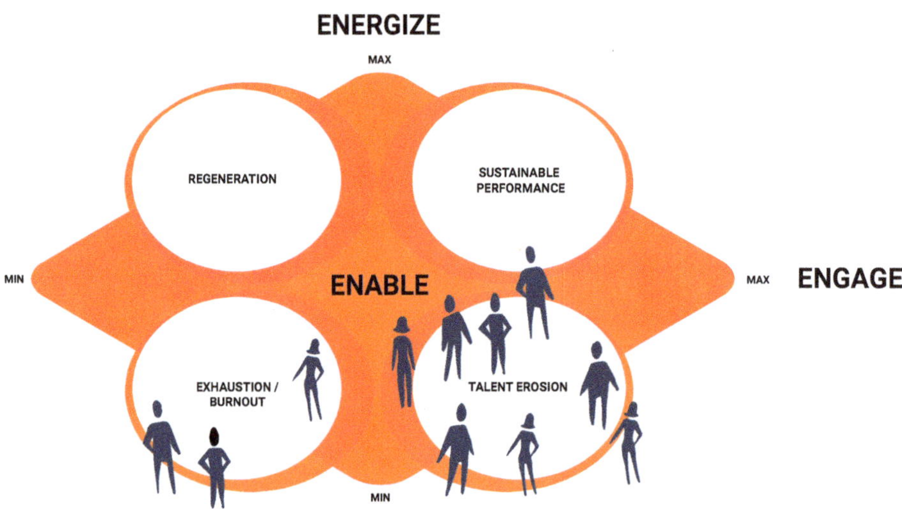

Although most team members were still highly engaged (if not over-engaged), they were overwhelmed by the crisis facing the organization. Many said that they felt powerless and not fully enabled to deal with the challenges they had been facing in the previous two years. Several told me that they were worried about their own or their colleagues' health, and were afraid that they might eventually burn out if things continued as they were. The team showed clear symptoms of chronic stress and exhaustion, including poor sleep, confusion, over-engagement, lack of focus, emotional dysfunction and drain, and an inability to make decisions.

In an effort to resolve the situation, a majority of the team had over-invested themselves and launched multiple projects and initiatives for which they lacked the resources. The team was operating in panic mode, and

Dealing with loss and grief

So, my coaching colleagues and I decided to set the business dimension aside for a while and instead focus on the human aspect. We started the first team workshop with a set of activities designed to get everyone together and engaged in the process. While doing that, our internal goal was to build enough psychological safety and trust in the group to proceed with the following session on unresolved grief.

Facilitating grief work with a group is a delicate exercise, because participants need to explore their emotions and vulnerabilities. As they do this, the group and the facilitators must create a strong secure base that can "hold the space" and keep all participants on safe ground. During this grief session, I asked the team to form a circle and to pass around a stone while expressing how they felt about what had happened over the last 1-2 years, and how they felt now. I chose a stone weighing 2-3 kilograms, so that the team members could feel its weight but still hold it easily.

The stone served as a transition object and enabled participants literally to unload emotions and grieve organizational "traumas" that they had not processed

until then. A lot of tears flowed as the team members expressed the pain of letting some of their colleagues go, and grieved that the organization was no longer what it used to be. Some expressed their guilt, anger, sadness, and worries. After that painful but necessary exercise, we could feel huge relief in the group as we symbolically placed the stone in the center of the circle.

Doing grief work had released tremendous energy from within the team. Energy that had been locked up was suddenly flowing freely again.

A few moments later, people started to smile. They were expressing things that they were grateful for, why being part of this NGO mattered so much to them, and why the organization was close to their heart. They started to re-connect with their hopes and with the common purpose that was holding them together as a team.

The team was now ready to work on the business dimension, but before that everyone needed some rest.

Leveraging the 18 team sustainability drivers

After a good night's sleep, we opened the following morning's session with a group meditation. Toward the end of it, I invited the team to consider what they would need to unlock their current situation.

To kick-start the process, I asked the group to look at all 18 team sustainability drivers and reflect on how these could help them to solve their organization's current challenges. The team then began to establish priorities regarding how they could best leverage those different dimensions in their new context.

The team chose to work first on the *Common Purpose & Vision* driver. They quickly concluded that despite the current crisis, they were totally clear as to **why** they existed as an organiza-tion. The very essence of their common purpose, their raison d'être, was still valid and had not changed as a result of the challenges they were now facing.

But to survive the crisis, the team had to fundamentally revisit **what** they were doing and **how** they were delivering those services to their target audience. In that respect, the team was following Simon Sinek's advice that organizations need to *Start with Why*[36] before moving into the what and how.

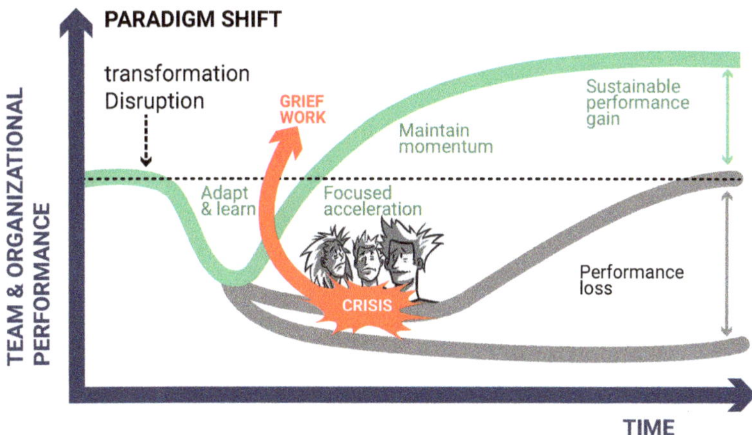

---

[36]Simon Sinek, Start with Why: How Great Leaders Inspire Everyone to Take Action, Reprint edition (New York, NY: Portfolio, 2011).

The NGO had to look out of the box to reinvent itself and quickly find a better fit with its new environment. So, the team took a brave approach and significantly challenged the status quo, with the aim of finding creative new ways to deliver value and make an impact with fewer resources.

The team decided to completely reshape their vision of who they would like to be as an organization. They redefined their organization's vision and mission and the nature of the partnerships they would like to have with key stakeholders. They proposed repositioning the NGO as a "center of expertise," which implied changing how they worked with regional partners. And they created a new five-year strategic roadmap focused on fewer streams of activities and projects, in line with the organization's reduced resources.

While working on *Common Purpose & Vision*, the team identified six drivers that required priority attention:

● A first set of four drivers were related to the NGO's strategic repositioning. These were *Strategy, Roadmap, & Priorities*, *Stakeholder & Risk Management*, *Customer Experience*, and *Innovation & Value Creation*.

● The other two drivers (*Work-Life & Energy Management*, and *Psychological Safety & Trust*) were more related to the team's energy and well-being. Most of the team members were in the Talent Erosion and Exhaustion/Burnout zones, which was clearly not sustainable. They also said that psychological safety and trust in the organization's leadership urgently needed restoring after having progressively declined during the last 12-18 months as a result of the project cuts, staff reductions, and financial uncertainty.

We then placed the *Common Purpose & Vision* driver in the center of the big rope circle and arranged the other six drivers immediately around it (see below).

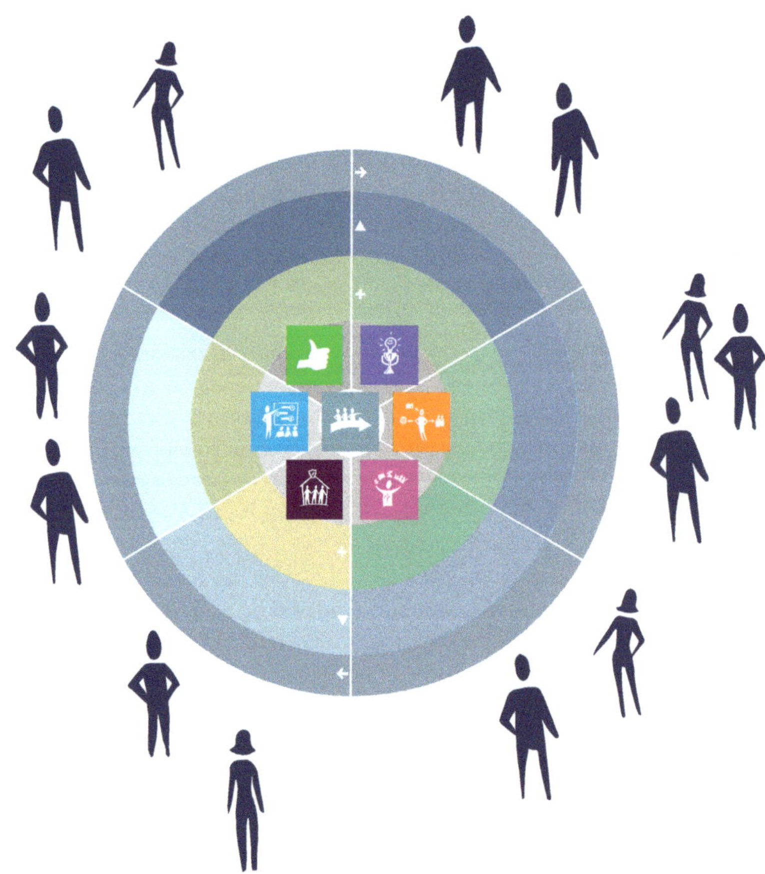

Next, we ran a collective brainstorming session with the team. By the end of it, the entire team had co-developed a clear picture of what they could do to influence their current context. Everyone came out of this exercise with a shared understanding of *what* the NGO's new strategy would be and *why* such actions were needed to move out of the crisis.

Implementation, follow-up, and outcomes

After this first workshop, the team needed a few weeks to refine their new strategy and come up with an integrated approach to present to the board for approval.

The NGO's new vision, mission, and five-year strategic roadmap were swiftly accepted by the board. Our next step was to define in more detail how we would coach the team as it started to implement the new strategy at the operational level.

In parallel with the group workshops, we had also coached the leadership team in order to make sure that they maintained a participative approach in working through the next steps with the team. It was important for us to follow the progress being made in terms of both content and teamwork.

This first implementation phase helped to clarify roles, responsibilities, and workflows in the new organizational model. Throughout this process, we were mindful of how mutual trust and psychological safety evolved in the group.

In the following 12-18 months, the new strategy started to yield positive outcomes, some of which are highlighted in the figure below:

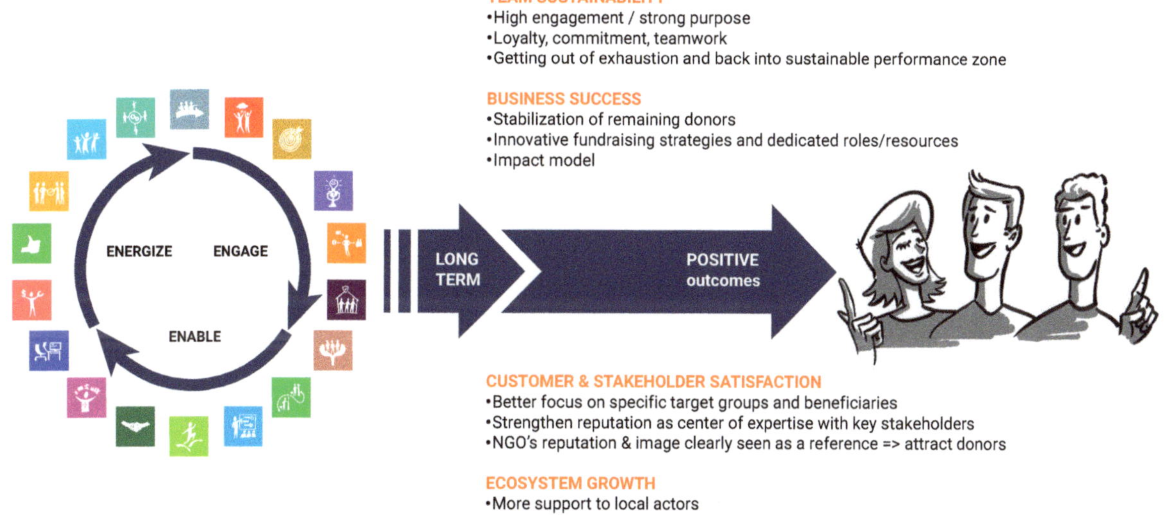

This case study is a great example of how the collective intelligence framework and the 18 team sustainability drivers can work hand in hand. By combining initial grief work with these tools, the NGO team was able to reaffirm its purpose and choose the right drivers on which to focus its acceleration efforts. The team reinvented itself and regained momentum with a new strategy to pursue a more sustainable organizational future. As a result, it quickly got out of its crisis and back into high-performance teamwork.

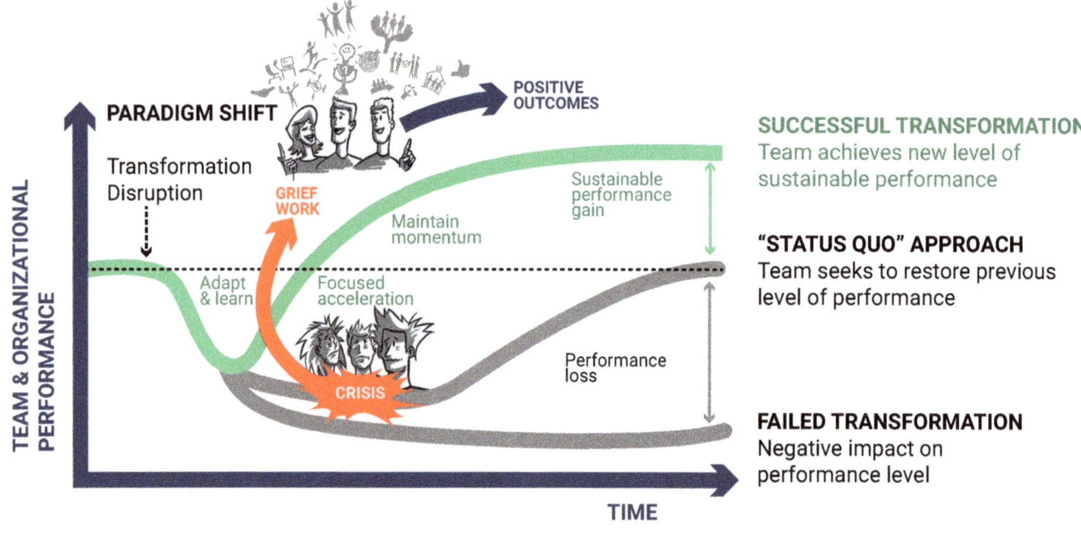

Case study No. 2: Organizational development of an industry-leading firm

This case study concerns a supply chain and customer service team within a leading international firm in a specialized business-to-business industry. The customer service department covers operations in different regions, and has teams located in different countries.

Initial situation/context

Three years previously, the company had launched a global cross-functional initiative with major implications for several departments, including manufacturing, supply chain, customer service, IT, and finance. It initially planned to complete the project within two years, but didn't allocate enough resources in the development phase. The firm had therefore extended the timeline – initially by six months and later by a further 12 months, meaning that the project was now scheduled to last almost twice as long as originally planned.

During that time, the customer service team had provided flawless customer support despite struggling with numerous changes to its internal platforms. The team was now in an advanced state of exhaustion, and a major internal conflict had erupted two weeks previously between the team leader and a few team members. In addition, the company's leadership was now planning to announce a further delay to the cross-functional initiative and a reorganization of the project team. The head of customer service and HR director were afraid that the upcoming announcement would be too much for the team, and could have irreversible consequences on both a human and business level.

Creating a safe space to enable team dialogue

Like the NGO in the first case study, this team was also going through a crisis but for different reasons. In this case, chronic stress and fatigue had triggered an inter-personal conflict that had polarized the team and blocked dialogue.

Our priority was therefore to re-establish a safe space where true dialogue could resume. This time, instead of asking team members to pass a stone to one another in a circle while expressing their feelings about recent events, we decided to use a Russian *matryoshka* nesting doll. Its softer, wooden structure and the symbolic act of unfolding the successive layers invited the participants to reconnect with their inner feelings. As the *matryoshka* passed from hand to hand, team members started to express their vulnerability, and the space progressively filled with empathy and mutual understanding.

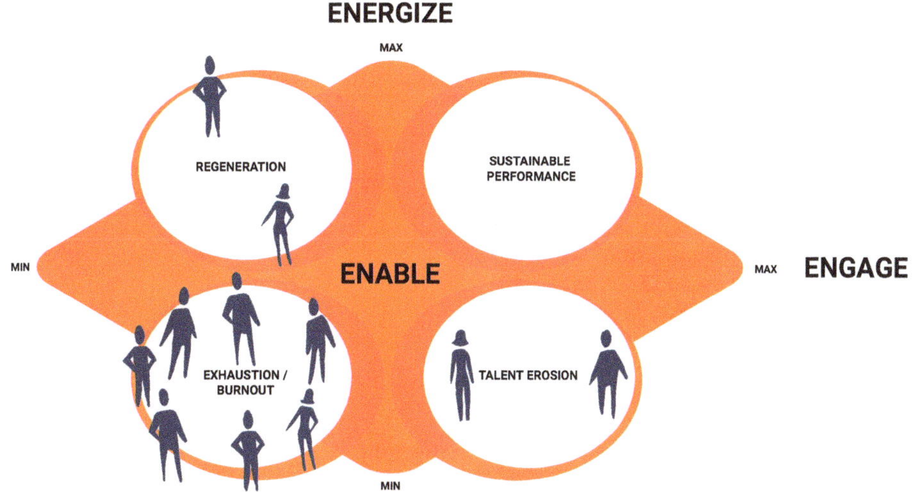

True dialogue was now possible. And as we continued with the session, the team raised several important points.

Leveraging the 18 team sustainability drivers

The first thing that emerged was that the team had always been and was still extremely committed to providing the best possible customer service. So, the team identified *Customer Experience* as one of their core values and decided to put it in the center of the collective intelligence circle. They also placed this driver at the center of the collective intelligence framework to serve as a focal point.

As we continued, it became clear that the team perceived a significant lack of support from the company's leadership. They felt that they had been put under constant pressure in the previous 2-3 years, with no signs of recognition for their efforts. The successive project delays had conveyed a negative message of them being poor performers while they were doing their best to cope with the situation. The team members therefore thought that *Supportive Leadership* and *Recognition & Reward* could be strong drivers to invert the current team and project dynamics, and decided to include them in Circle 1.

The next two drivers that emerged were *Conflict & Feedback Management* and *Psychological Safety & Trust*. Strong tensions had arisen between the different departments involved in the cross-functional project. During the workshop, some team members had the courage to report a series of recurrent dysfunctional behaviors – including people slamming doors and shouting at each other – that had contributed to creating a climate of fear and anxiety. Such behaviors were clearly not aligned with the company's values and had to be addressed urgently by senior management. In addition, interpersonal conflicts had recently surfaced within the customer service team itself. The team could not afford to let these internal clashes deteriorate further, and decided that the *Conflict & Feedback Management* driver needed immediate focus.

Some team members shared that they were feeling highly vulnerable in this context, and feared for their health and family-work balance. They had been over-focusing on their work and neglecting other areas of their lives over the previous 2-3 years. So, the team decided to make *Work-Life & Energy Management* one of their priorities on the circular collective intelligence mat.

Finally, the team established that project delays were mostly related to a lack of *Resources & Know-How* at operational and project-management level. Although this issue had already been escalated to the company's leadership, they had not yet addressed it properly. The team wanted to brainstorm new ways to resolve this issue, because it was at the root of their current challenges. So, they made it the sixth related driver around the center of the circle.

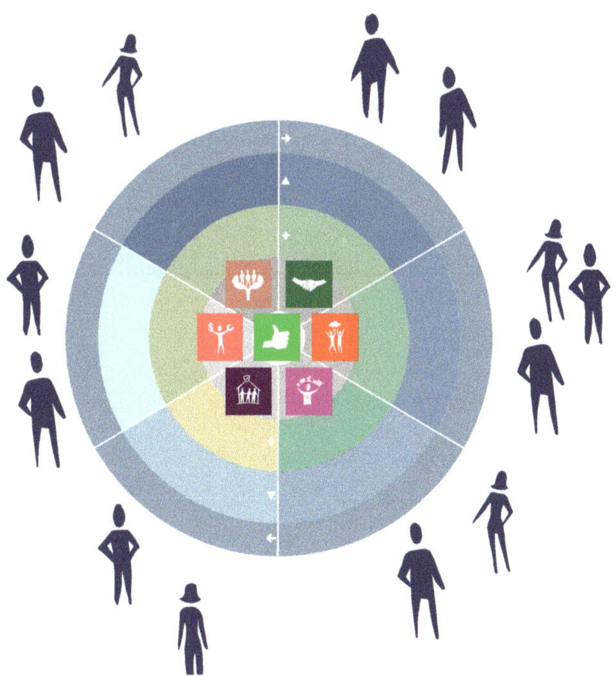

The collective brainstorming session proved extremely useful in remobilizing the team's energy toward positive outcomes and common goals in a challenging context. The team had been taken hostage by the cross-functional project, and its members were locked into a state where they felt they had no leverage to shape the future.

Stephen Covey's model of the three circles of control, influence, and concern[37] helps to illustrate the dynamics at play in this situation. The team was clearly under pressure as a result of developments at an organizational level (i.e. within their Circle of Concern). They were over-focusing on those external factors and had become reactive and passive, and hence more vulnerable to feeling overwhelmed and exhausted. Instead, they urgently needed to find new ways to mobilize their energy and channel their actions toward factors that they could directly leverage both individually and collectively as a team. In other words, they needed to focus on their Circles of Control and Influence.

CIRCLES OF INFLUENCE

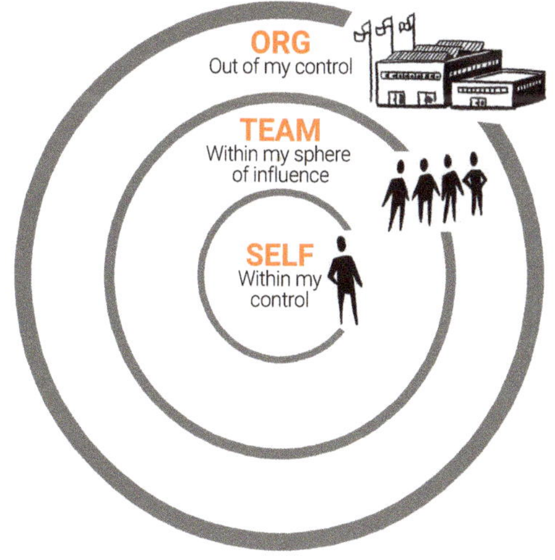

---

[37]Covey, The 7 Habits of Highly Effective People.

Given the many uncertainties surrounding the project, it was all the more important that the customer service team had a clear strategy and roadmap for what they wanted to achieve together.

Implementation, follow-up, and outcomes

The team identified many practical steps that they could take to gain more grip on the situation and restore a positive team dynamic. Many of these are easily transferable to other teams. For example, they decided to:

● Establish team norms to signal and regulate emotions and conflicts. The team decided on a common "code" to signal situations that required a debrief, and agreed with the HR department that the latter would play a mediator role to facilitate such sessions.

● Have a common training involving the team and their key stakeholders on how to use non-violent communication to give and receive insightful feedback in the workplace.

One of our immediate follow-up actions – previously agreed with the team – was to flag the dysfunctions induced by the cross-functional project to executives and the CEO. Although we had done good work with the customer service team, senior leadership intervention was clearly required to restore a more sustainable workplace environment that was aligned with the company's values and reputation.

While conducting this higher-level follow-up, we partnered with the firm's HR department to set up frequent debriefs with the customer service team in the 3-6 months following the initial workshop. We wanted to make sure that the team was getting enough support and building enough resilience.

The company's executives then acted immediately to put the cross-functional project back on track, enforce the use of non-violent communication within the organization (in line with its values and desired group norms and leadership behaviors), and provide more resources and support to the team. But some challenges linked to the broader economic context and the company's suppliers were not

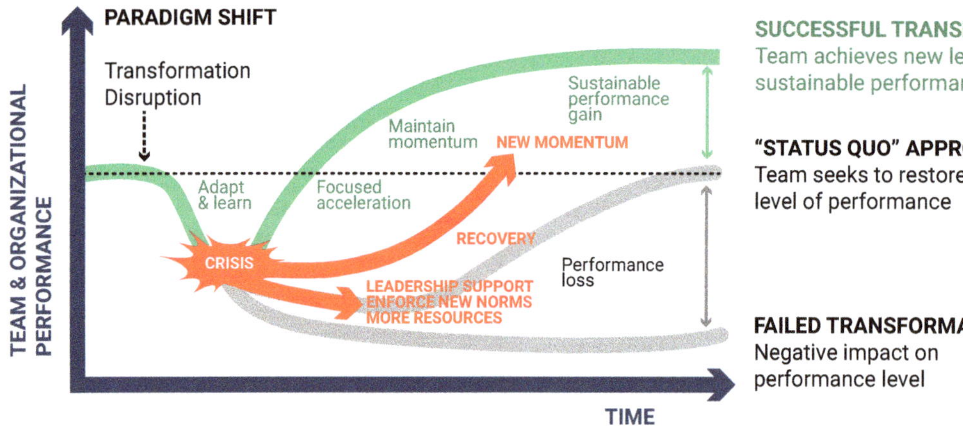

● Proactively distribute kudos to recognize and value each other's contributions and positive behaviors. The team brainstormed a few "gamified approaches" to boost recognition and reward both within and beyond their group. The aim was to develop games that help to reinforce group norms and behaviors and make it simple and fun to recognize other team members' efforts.

entirely in senior management's hands, and needed another 3-6 months to evolve positively.

The customer service team itself was back on track within a few weeks, but it took up to 9-12 months for all its members to fully recover the life balance and personal energy they wanted. Following this recovery period, the team has regained its resilience, strengthened its internal cohesion, and created new momentum.

Case study No. 3: Development and reorganization of an HR team

port. Although the team was dealing with a significant workload, they had the capacity to handle most of their colleagues' requests to support swift business operations. Most of the team members felt enabled, energized, and engaged in their work, and placed themselves in the Sustainable Performance quadrant (see diagram).

The HR team had a reputation for doing good work, and the director wanted to dedicate the first team workshop

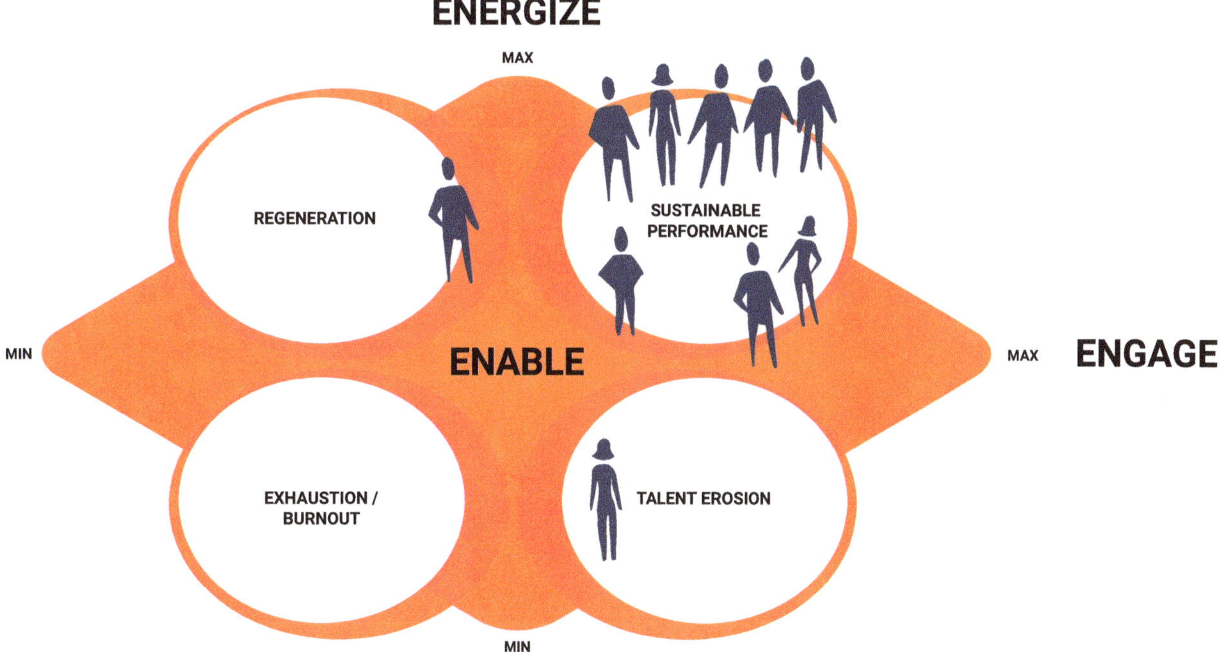

This case study concerns the human resources team of a fast-growing organization. The organization had enjoyed a five-year-long boom, and as a result the HR department had doubled in size within the last two years. The HR director had been with the organization since day one. She was expecting her team to stabilize at its current size, and – now that all key members were on board – saw an opportunity to forge a strong team spirit within her high-performing unit.

Initial situation/context

In recent months, the organization had created new HR roles and functions, and new people had joined the team to help meet the increasing need for HR sup-

to seeing how the new fully staffed group could further improve their service level. Everything seemed to be under control, and my colleagues and I were anticipating a relatively smooth ride as we prepared the first workshop with the group. But the initial teamwork session quickly revealed a few breaches in the team dynamic.

Confronting tension

We had agreed to start the workshop by asking the team to map out the different activities in the talent management cycle in which they were involved (see figure on next page). The team's objective was to identify the key interaction points where HR was delivering value to the business, and see how they could better serve their internal customers at each point in this process.

As we started to work through the talent cycle, many areas of friction and disagreement started to surface between the HR team's three subunits, and a few team members became progressively upset. They adopted a more rigid body language, and became verbally more assertive, if not aggressive, toward some of their colleagues.

The HR director then intervened and asked her team to avoid personal attacks on each other. As we continued, it became obvious that the team needed to deal with internal conflicts that it had avoided until then and were about to burst out during this workshop.

At this point, I realized that the team was probably still in its *forming* phase and was reluctant to engage in *storming*[38], where conflict arises as team members begin to establish their place. As is common with HR professionals, most of the team members were trying to maintain peace and harmony, but it was time for the team to confront its areas of tension. Otherwise, the team would risk drifting into conflict avoidance and artificial harmony, eventually resulting in a toxic dynamic that would strongly hinder its performance.

I shared my observations with the group, and invited them to unpack their areas of tension and safely voice their concerns. The team quickly concluded that in order to serve their internal customers better, they had to address several of their own internal drivers.

Leveraging the 18 team sustainability drivers

To stimulate interactions and maximize participants' engagement, we combined brainstorming sessions in smaller groups with idea consolidation in plenary discussions. During these exercises, the team reflected on how the 18 drivers could help them to overcome their current challenges and further improve performance.

---

[38]Tuckman, "Developmental Sequence in Small Groups."

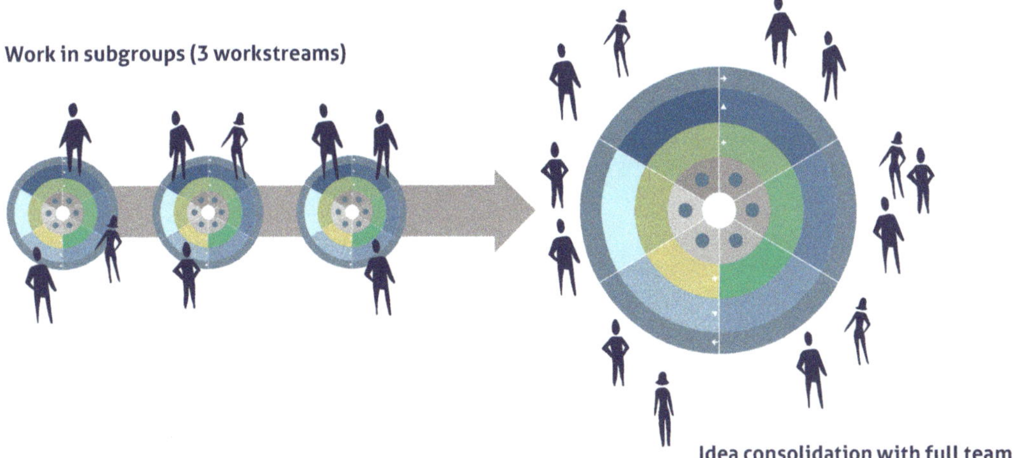

The team decided to place *Customer Experience* at the center of the collective intelligence mat in order to focus on how they could better collectively serve internal customers within the organization. They identified different segments of customers, along with their specific needs and the service level required at each phase of the talent cycle. The team's goal was to consistently deliver a great customer experience each time an individual, team, department head, or even the executive leadership team or board of directors needed support from HR.

The team then identified the drivers they wanted to place in Circle 1 to support that goal.

● First, the team members realized that although they were all doing their best to serve the business, they were lacking a clear *Strategy, Roadmap, & Priorities* for doing that collectively.

● The team acknowledged that its rapid growth had resulted in clearly suboptimal work processes and workflows, with numerous redundancies and a lack of clarity on roles and responsibilities. This resulted in delays, inefficiencies, and frustrations for the team and their customers. The team had recently introduced three main workstreams in order to bring more structure to the overall group, and decided that the *Clear Roles & Processes* driver would certainly be one of their top Circle 1 priorities.

● They also concluded that part of the team was probably still resisting the changes and role shifts resulting from the onboarding of new people. Some were also avoiding collaboration and trying to reduce their interactions with some of the newer team members. The team made it clear that this could not continue. Delivering the best HR services required the whole team to be on board, which meant quickly reaching a high level of interdependability and teamwork. They therefore also included the *Enthusiasm & Positive Attitude Toward Change* and *Dependability & Teamwork* drivers in Circle 1.

● Finally, like the customer service team in case study No. 2, the group decided that it had to address *Conflict & Feedback Management* and *Psychological Safety & Trust*. In this case, the HR team's conflicts were more covert and not expressed, so we had to establish group norms regarding its members' tolerance of conflict. Because most of them tended to be naturally conflict-avoidant, the team needed more encouragement and a greater level of psychological safety to address its areas of tension collectively.

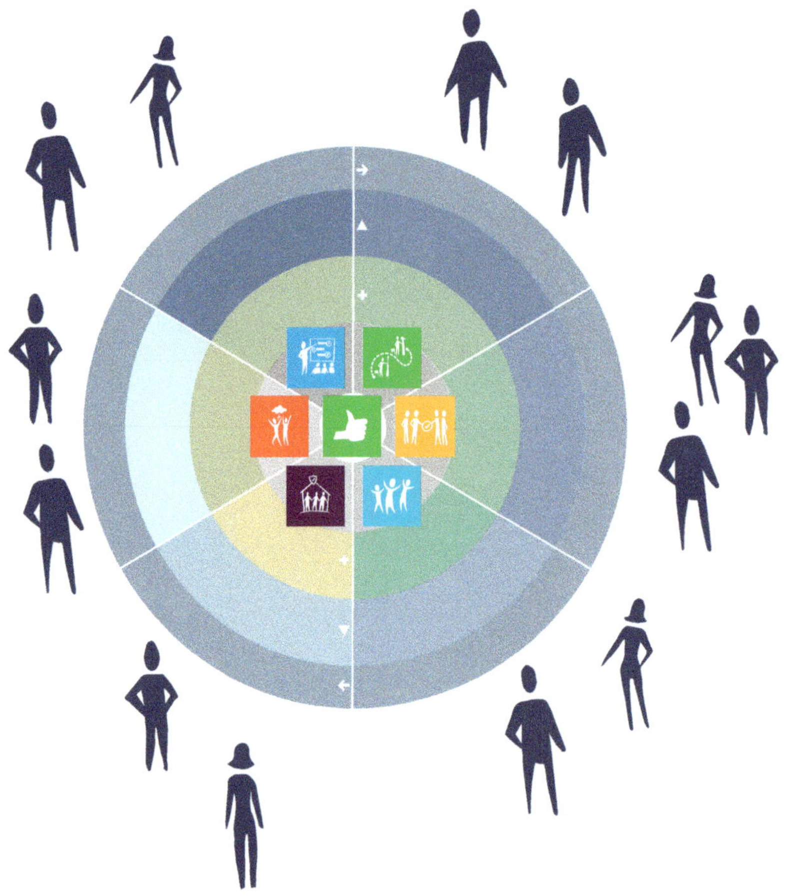

Implementation, follow-up, and outcomes

After those initial readjustments, the HR team subsequently developed well and continues to evolve relatively favorably. It operates autonomously and needs less intense follow-ups than the teams in the first two case studies. We usually have a follow-up workshop every 6-9 months to maintain the team's positive momentum and sustain its high performance over time.

Four keys to successful team development

I now want to zoom out of the specific case studies and outline some best practices that I usually recommend for successfully developing sustainable teams and organizations.

In particular, team development:

- is context-driven

- combines structure with agility

- is going hybrid, and

- is a marathon, not a sprint.

Team development is context-driven

When designing coaching interventions aimed at building sustainable teams, it is vital to remember that the team's context or environment drives its development needs, and not vice versa.

As the pyramid to the right makes clear, the team's **context** defines the required **transformations**, which in turn define team **coaching needs**. Team coaching activities should always be subordinated to the team's context. Organizations that use team coaching proactively regard it as a strategic resource to guide their teams effectively through important transformations. Likewise, sustainable teams decide to request team coaching ahead of time, and make it an integral part of their organization's strate-

gy for achieving sustainable high performance. When used properly, team coaching can greatly accelerate team transformations and ensure a best fit with the overall context.

As Roger Schwarz[39] has argued, "effective teams don't just happen – you design them. And two of the most important elements of that design are a.) the degree to which team members are interdependent – where they need to rely on each other to accomplish the team task, and b.) how you'll actually coordinate that interdependence."

---

[39]Roger M. Schwarz, Smart Leaders, Smarter Teams: How You and Your Team Get Unstuck to Get Results, 1st edition (San Francisco, CA: Jossey-Bass, 2013).

That's why team-building activities bring value only when they are part of a well-thought-through coaching journey that addresses the team's important challenges in a structured and coherent way.

As in the previous case studies, any sustainable team development project starts by analyzing the **team's context** and defining what the team, its leaders, and its HR business partners expect from the initiative. During that initial phase, all stakeholders need to develop a shared vision of the challenges that will be on the team's agenda in the upcoming 6-18 months (or longer, if possible), and consequently arrive at a shared understanding of why team **transformations** are needed.

Only then can we start to map the team's **coaching journey**, and define what we want the team to achieve in which timeframe, and how we will make this happen. Designing a team coaching journey is similar to defining the mix of a learning program: the key is to identify which tools and resources are relevant in the particular context, and then to combine them to create maximum value and a transformational experience for the participants.

Elements that I like to build into team coaching journeys include:

● Diversified team meeting formats, such as workshops, debriefing circles, stand-up meetings, and team snapshots via video conference. I always make sure to adapt the format to the meeting's purpose and desired outcomes.

● Various frameworks to leverage collective intelligence, structure and prioritize ideas, and facilitate decision-making. These include the collective intelligence framework, the 18 team sustainability drivers, a stakeholder map, and Business Model Canvas[40].

● Structured team feedback exercises (e.g. one-on-one, one-to-many, or many-to-one feedback, and 360° developmental feedback).

● Experiential learning through different formats, including team challenges, serious games, role plays, videos, TED talks, case studies, and readings.

● In-depth exploration through personality-type profiling, combined with debriefing with specialized practitioners.

● Individual coaching and/or mentoring with internal or external coaches and mentors. Sometimes, peer-coaching tandems or groups can also help to leverage an organization's internal resources while strengthening interpersonal bonds and mutual trust.

Facilitators designing a team coaching journey should not become dogmatic about a specific approach, or push for a technique that they are more familiar or comfortable with. Instead, I prefer team coaches to scout for the best possible mix of tools and expertise to catalyze the team's transformation in the given context. We should always adapt each team coaching program to ensure a best-fit approach.

Team development combines structure with agility

Team coaching is a dynamic and interactive process, and striking the right balance between structure and agility is key to implementing programs successfully.

Because teams frequently change their priorities in today's VUCA environment, team coaching requires a constant high level of agility. But total flexibility does not have to mean total chaos, provided that there is a strong underlying structure upon which everyone can stand. In that respect, team coaching is similar to playing jazz, where each song has a predefined canvas or structure upon which musicians can swiftly improvise and adapt to what the other band members do.

---

[40]Alexander Osterwalder and Yves Pigneur, Business Model Generation: A Handbook for Visionaries, Game Changers, and Challengers, 1st edition (Hoboken, NJ: John Wiley and Sons, 2010).

That is why my colleagues and I start every team coach-ing intervention by establishing its workflow, structure, and high-level roadmap. First, we map the team coaching journey with its successive steps. We outline the different workshops and plan the sequence of resources and tools we intend to use during the project. Then we capture all that into a high-level visual roadmap. Similarly, for each specific team workshop we map the different exercises and the workflow along with the expected outcomes.

But once we go live in the implementation phase, it is essential to feel what is happening in the team at both a conscious and unconscious level. If the team dynamic shifts, it makes little sense to stick to a predetermined plan. Instead of forcing our approach onto the team, we need to be agile and adapt in order to be in tune with where the team stands at that moment. This should ensure *resonant* instead of *dissonant* relationships and interactions between the team and facilitators.

I find the **seven-step sequence** below useful for maintain-ing an appropriate mix of structure and agility during team coaching interventions. Throughout the coaching journey, the facilitators' role is to:

Taken together, the seven steps create a continuous pos-itive feedback loop that mimics the philosophy of agile project management.

Team development is going hybrid

The rapid migration to digital technologies triggered by the global COVID-19 pandemic during 2020 will most probably persist even as the world (hopefully) conquers the coronavirus and starts its economic recovery. After all, companies that have recently led the way in adopting flat-ter, fully agile organizational models have substantially improved both their pace of execution and productivity[41].

When governments around the world introduced lock-downs, many teams had to adapt almost overnight to working remotely. Remote working has increased by up to 75-80% in most professional and business-services orga-nizations during lockdowns, and is likely to remain above pre-crisis levels for some time.

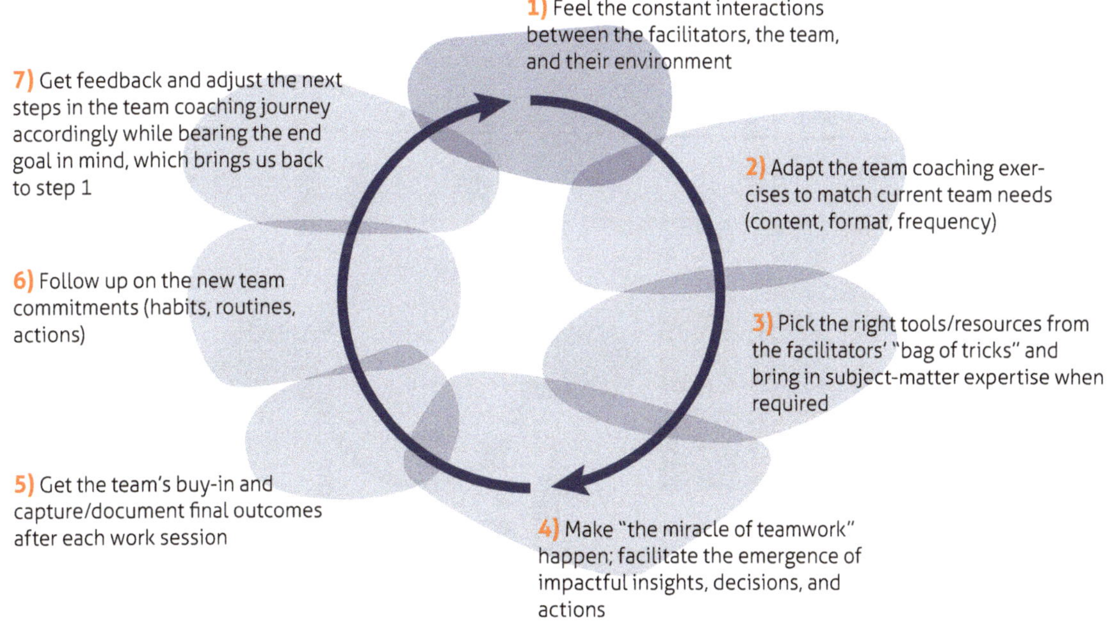

[41] "Digital Adoption through COVID-19 and beyond | McKinsey," 2020, https://www.mckinsey.com/business-functions/mckinsey-digital/our-insights/the-covid-19-recovery-will-be-digital-a-plan-for-the-first-90-days.

Among the many other changes it will induce, the pandemic will surely accelerate the shift toward more digital team development solutions. In fact, using *physical* and *digital* platforms in combination is a smart way to ensure higher impact and better follow-up on such programs.

Having team members physically present in the same room is a highly engaging teamwork format. For example, our illustrated cubes that physically represent and materialize the 18 team sustainability drivers are an extremely versatile and hands-on tool to facilitate interactive, high-performance teamwork. They provide a framework and structure, and invite teams and facilitators to be creative and agile in the way they use them. This format is also efficient, enabling teams to quickly identify their Circle 1 drivers, visualize their top priorities, vote on the best ideas, and agree on the most urgent actions.

Physical tools also serve as transfer objects that give life to abstract concepts and make intangible notions more tangible. The 18 driver cubes emphasize the fact that the team is doing team development work; in fact, they anchor it. And when the team brings the cubes back to their own office after the coaching workshops, they act as a useful reminder to follow up on ongoing actions. They also make team development efforts visible to others who pass by the team's office space, and communicate a positive image to people who interact with the team – including other teams, external visitors, and customers.

Team development work via digital platforms is less emotionally engaging, but is a must for remote teams and can be a powerful complement to traditional physical team meetings – especially given the ongoing pandemic. Digital workspaces offer a great way to document, keep track of, and update team actions according to their latest status. And for workshop follow-ups, digital platforms can be more efficient than in-person meetings. They are time- and cost-effective because team members can connect remotely instead of having to travel.

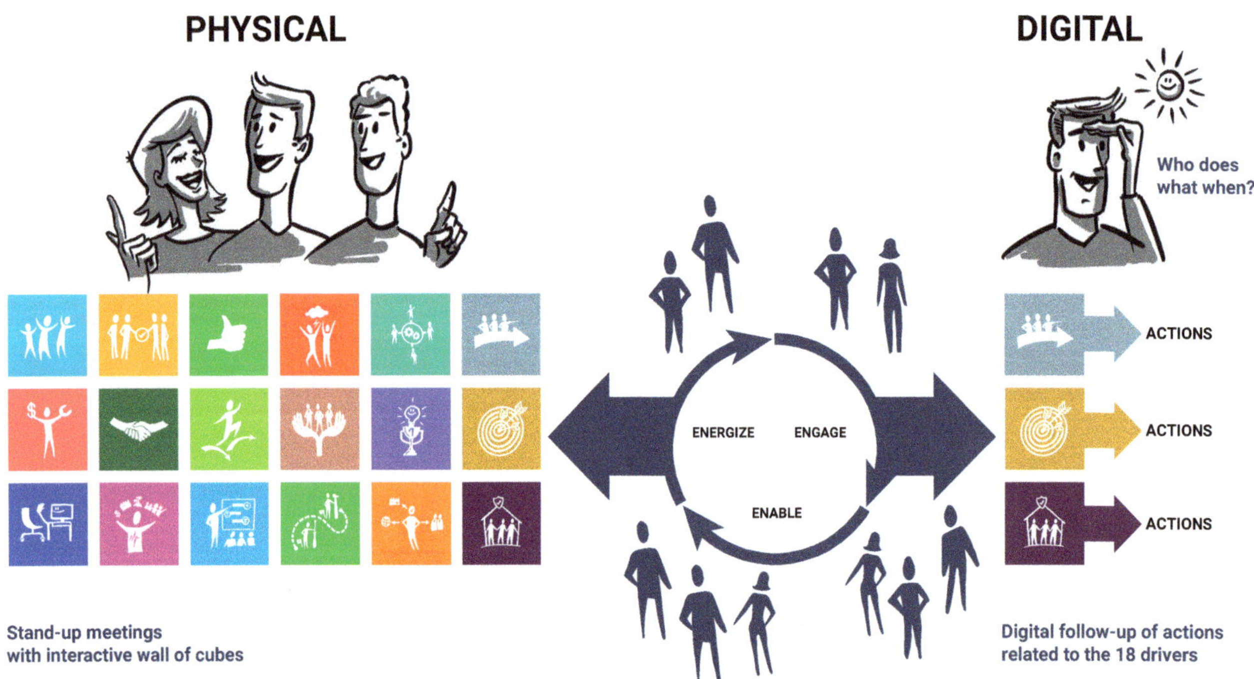

**Stand-up meetings
with interactive wall of cubes**

**Digital follow-up of actions
related to the 18 drivers**

Pros of a PHYSICAL platform *(the 18 driver cubes)*:

● Makes intangible notions tangible.

● Effective tool to facilitate group workshops (visually attractive, fun to work with, and engaging).

● Long-lasting impact after group workshops when the team places cubes in its work environment.

● Wall of cubes in the office can serve as an expression board to collect team suggestions and ideas.

● Can be used autonomously by the team after workshops to structure follow-up/stand-up meetings.

● Communication tool for internal and external visitors; can also be shared with other teams in the organization.

Pros of a DIGITAL platform:

● A must for remote teams.

● Offers a convenient way to capture and share information with remote teams, or with others who didn't participate in a team workshop.

● Structured way to document key decisions and follow up on action items identified by the team.

● Enables remote access and asynchronous work by all team members regardless of their location and time zone.

● Effective reporting tool with dynamic updates on the team's progress via dashboards etc.

Ideally, each team coaching program should integrate physical and digital tools thoughtfully, and seek synergies between them. Facilitators should avoid potential redundancies and inefficiencies, so that the different platforms complement each other nicely and add value to the overall program.

Team development is a marathon, not a sprint

Just as children don't grow into adults overnight, there is no quick-fix solution that instantly turns teams into sustainable teams. Yet, today's work environment seems to  demand immediate returns in everything we do, and I am shocked at how many leaders (and sometimes even HR professionals) are under pressure to obtain instant results from their team development efforts.

In my experience, trying to rush teams through important transformations will usually end up doing more harm than good. Human beings need time to process their thoughts and emotions and deal with changes.

Most leaders fail to realize that they are often one step ahead of their teams regarding transformations, especially when their organization has a top-down approach to dealing with change. Senior management might be ready to implement a change within their teams, but lower-level employees are not yet ready to make it happen. Leaders need to take a step back and give their teams time and space to process the changes.

That is why I prefer, whenever possible, to pace our team coaching interventions so that teams can "breathe" between two sessions. During the first phase of a team coaching program, we typically have a 2-3 month interval between consecutive workshops. In the second phase, once the team has become more autonomous, we can allow more space between follow-up sessions.

Although team workshops play an important role in catalyzing change, what happens in the intervals between them is even more important. As Anders Ericsson and other psychologists showed in their famous study of the role of deliberate practice in achieving expert performance[42], it takes about 10,000 hours, or approximately five full-time years, of structured practice to reach a level of excellence in any field of activity, such as tennis or music, for example.

Applying the same logic to team development explains why sustainable teams can develop only over time. Our role in team coaching is to provoke instant shifts in a team's consciousness that lead to immediate actions, *and* to ensure subsequent consistent follow-ups so that those shifts can translate into long-term benefits.

Throughout the team's development journey, team coaching interventions should be as limited as possible. They should help the team to stay on track as it develops and anchors new positive habits, but teams should not become dependent on their coaches – and coaches should not become substitutes for team leaders. Rather, their goal should be to promote and preserve a high level of autonomy in the teams they coach.

Over time, the team will integrate the underlying principles and tools used in coaching until these become new habits that are part of its modus operandi. This will lead to sustainable high performance in terms of team sustainability, business success, customer satisfaction, and ecosystem growth.

That, in a nutshell, is the logic of the integrated framework and impact model that I am sharing with you in this book.

<hr>

[42]Anders Ericsson, Ralf Krampe, and Clemens Tesch-Römer, "The Role of Deliberate Practice in the Acquisition of Expert Performance," Psychological Review 100 (July 1, 1993): 363–406, https://doi.org/10.1037//0033-295X.100.3.363.

KEY LEARNINGS

Part IV

1. Establishing a new culture of team development requires **buy-in from all stakeholders** within the organization, including and starting with **senior management**.

2. The success of any team development program depends heavily on the quality of its **preparation**. Remember the golden rule: 80% preparation, 20% execution.

3. For most organizations, building sustainable teams is a **paradigm shift**, and you should **expect resistance** during the implementation phase. Like in **Aïkido**, be ready to welcome the resistance and **deflect that energy** to drive the desired changes across the organization.

4. Team development today is **context-driven**, combines **structure with agility**, increasingly uses both **physical and digital platforms**, and is a **marathon, not a sprint**.

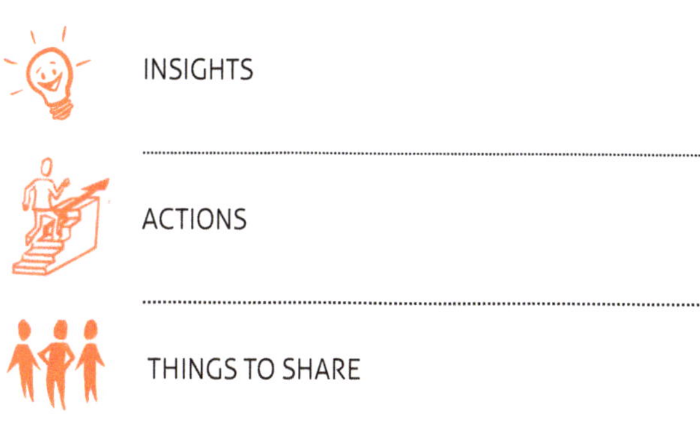

PART V – How to Leverage the 18 Team Sustainability Drivers

This section provides a catalogue of best practices and things to avoid when implementing each of the 18 drivers with your team. You can return to it whenever you or your colleagues need guidance on how to address a specific driver within your organization.

CONFLICT & FEEDBACK
MANAGEMENT

COMMUNICATION
TOOLS & PLATFORMS

COMMON
PURPOSE & VISION

SUPPORTIVE LEADERSHIP

INNOVATION &
VALUE CREATION

INSPIRING GOALS
SELF & TEAM

CLEAR ROLES
& PROCESSES

STAKEHOLDER
& RISK MANAGEMENT

PSYCHOLOGICAL
SAFETY & TRUST

COMMON PURPOSE & VISION

WHY IT MATTERS

Many teams keep themselves busy but are unclear about their final destination and, more importantly, about why they do what they do. As Henry David Thoreau wrote, "It's not enough to be busy, so are the ants. The question is, what are we busy about?" So, before you embark on a new journey with a team, you must clarify why you exist as a team and what your common purpose is. What is special about the team, and how does it create value? What special products, solutions, or services will this team deliver better, faster, and more sustainably than its individual members could do on their own?

THINGS TO DO

● **Start by identifying your *Why*[43]**. Make sure that your team is 100% clear about why they do what they do. Take the time to identify your common purpose and make it explicit: why does your team and organization exist? Why do you get out of bed in the morning? And why should anyone care? As Simon Sinek says, "it all starts with Why." When adversity strikes, your *Why* is both a strong anchor and a powerful glue that holds your team together.

[43]Sinek, Start with Why.

● **Make your *Why* alive, visible, audible, and even tangible.** Reinforce it whenever possible. Use different formats to communicate your *Why* both internally and externally. For example, formalize your team's purpose, vision, and mission in a team charter, video, mission statement, or any other type of collective artwork that can materialize and anchor a shared vision.

● **Make your vision as clear, specific, and attractive as possible.** The clearer you are about where you are going, the easier it will be to motivate your team to work toward this goal. A compelling vision enables leaders to anticipate an exciting future and, when communicated confidently to the team, provides a rallying motto that energizes everyone to accomplish big things.

● **Use your *Why* to create a sense of real commitment and attachment to a higher purpose.** This will help everyone to visualize how their contributions can add up to achieving an overarching common goal. When setting individual and departmental objectives, teams should always link them to the shared vision in order to avoid working in silos. People should still *feel* that they are all interdependent and belong to the same ecosystem. A strong common purpose should drive them to collaborate with others, because they will realize that they are all working toward the same goal.

● **Make sure that your purpose and vision statement resonates with your team's deeper values, aspirations, and intrinsic motivations,** and check that individual team members are aligned with it. When people with similar interests come together around a shared vision, the collective energy automatically shoots up. And when a team focuses on a shared purpose and mission, success means the same for everyone in it.

THINGS TO AVOID

● **Developing a vision statement that seems too nebulous, abstract, or idealistic.** People in your organization will likely have a hard time trusting your leadership and adhering to a vision that projects an overly vague future state.

● **Thinking that your purpose-vision-mission statements are just high-level concepts** that are either not worth the effort, not important, or do not add value to the organization. Leaders who focus only on deliverables and neglect the *Why* will fail to instill a sense of purpose in their teams, and will probably struggle to get the best performance from them.

● **Doing this exercise just to "tick the box."** You risk failing to connect with your team's deeper values and true purpose, and may end up with a vision statement that is too generic and does not resonate with their core motivations.

● **The solo approach.** People differ widely in terms of what is meaningful to them. If you convey a purpose that is meaningful only to you, there's a good chance that you'll leave the majority of your team uninspired. If you try to define purpose according to your own point of view, you limit your thinking and fail to engage others in the process.

● **Outlining your team's purpose during the team kick-off and then forgetting about it.** This is a big discount factor and signals that you are not truly living and standing behind your team's purpose. Instead, you should regularly engage with others to generate ideas for how your team can live according to its purpose. Frequently reminding team members of their common purpose is a powerful way to anchor shared goals, mobilize energy, and reinforce everyone's buy-in.

SUPPORTIVE LEADERSHIP

WHY IT MATTERS

I regard supportive leadership as a *sine qua non* for organizations that want to build sustainable teams. Supportive leaders are willing to focus on identifying what changes and support are required to ensure the well-being of their team. They also alleviate any unnecessary obstacles so that the team can perform to a high standard. A leader's ability to help and support a team (without being a "rescuer") is one of the fundamental pillars that will contribute to the team's success. Ideally, as George Kohlrieser emphasizes when discussing secure base leadership[44], leaders should provide the right mix of support (care) and positive challenge (dare) throughout all phases of team development. This is key to ensuring that as many team members as possible are in the right "state" and operate in the Sustainable Performance quadrant of my model.

THINGS TO DO

● **Promote a culture of supportive leadership throughout the organization,** including via mentoring, coaching, and 360° feedbacks for leaders. Leaders should be there for others, and the senior leadership team also needs to support each other, providing help and a boost when needed.

---

[44]Kohlrieser, Goldsworthy, and Coombe, Care to Dare.

● **Have board members and executives model and practice supportive leadership at all times.** Leaders should make themselves available and seek to empower everyone in the organization. The goal should be to enable people to improve their skills and talent until they can handle tasks with minimal supervision. Leaders should learn to behave as enablers and not rescuers with their teams.

● **Create an environment where people can take ownership and try out new things.** A supportive leader is able to accept mistakes, is accountable, and does not blame their team or criticize its work in front of others. He or she encourages people, and has a relationship with their teams that fosters an open dialogue. This enables team members to feel safe by learning from their mistakes in order to improve.

● **Give leaders opportunities to train, practice, and develop** their emotional intelligence, compassion, and empathy (caring), as well as their ability to challenge teams constructively (daring). HR and senior executives should provide common guidelines on which supportive leadership behaviors are expected, and explain how coaching and mentoring can bring value to the organization.

● **Promote a two-way dialogue where teams can express their needs,** including what support they require from their leadership. Leaders should be clear on how to act upon the needs outlined by the team. They can build trust and loyalty with their teams by following up diligently and consistently on agreed actions and also by clearly saying no to expectations that cannot be met.

THINGS TO AVOID

● **Dominant leadership,** which results in teams being under too much pressure and lacking support. In the worst-case scenario, a leader may become abusive and belittle people around them, using foul language, threats, or coercion. Such behavior fuels a culture of bullying and harassment, and should not be tolerated at any level of any organization.

● **Displaying a lack of interest in supporting and mentoring others.** Leaders sometimes negatively affect a team through their indifference, or their excessive self-promotion and self-interest. Supportive leaders should take time to nurture others and help them to develop their own career tracks. Otherwise, team members will feel stale and will not work to their full potential.

● **Being unwilling to listen to feedback.** A leader's repeated reluctance to hear or respond to others' meaningful concerns can lead to many conflicts and problems down the line, as well as to employee dissatisfaction, resentment, and attrition. Unfortunately, some leaders emphasize their own wishes and ideas instead of being receptive, supportive, and open to what their colleagues have to offer.

● **Being selective and unfair,** and offering supportive leadership to only a cherry-picked handful of team members. Mentoring opportunities should be communicated and distributed fairly, which requires leaders to have a strong ethical core that guides how they work with the people around them. They need to care about values such as fairness, social justice, equitable behavior, empathy, and humanism.

● **Being a "pleaser" leader who says yes to all the team's needs** but does not clearly commit to providing support, and does not consistently follow up on actions. In the worst cases, leaders may pretend to support their team members but then expose them to criticism when they themselves are under pressure.

RESOURCES & KNOW-HOW

WHY THEY MATTER

Having the right level of resources and know-how will help your team to handle the challenges ahead. New technologies are disrupting every industry, and organizations must rapidly adapt their tools, skills, and knowledge to cope with these changes. Digital transformation is driving rapid evolutions in the way teams, organizations, customers, and stakeholders share data and cooperate. To work smarter, teams need to be up to date with the latest digital workplace innovations. Besides traditional resources such as people, money, and equipment, teams in the knowledge-based economy need access to the latest know-how in their field of expertise. Does your team have the tools it needs to accomplish its mission?

THINGS TO DO

● **Empower teams with sufficient resources and know-how.** Ask them to identify which new skills, tools, and resources they think they need to succeed in their mission. Identify any gaps early on, ideally prior to the team kick-off or otherwise shortly afterward. Consider involving additional team members, and/or making expertise available through consultants who can work with the team on an ad hoc basis.

- **Make time and space for learning, and create a culture that rewards continuous learning.** Leaders should see opportunities to advance their teams' skills as a wise investment. They should not only actively encourage team members to learn new things through special projects or new assignments, but also ensure that this fresh know-how spreads rapidly within teams and across the organization.

- **Encourage a scouting mindset** to explore and test new technologies and see how they could help teams advance their work. Teams should follow emerging trends in different areas that can improve their performance and make their life easier, such as new hardware, equipment, and collaborative digital platforms.

- **Use blended learning to maximize options,** such as reading materials, courses and conferences, job shadowing, mentoring, and coaching. Consider every team member and situation. In-person learning allows for hands-on application and collaboration, while on-demand tools offer flexibility and enable people to learn at their own pace. Combining the two can help you achieve your learning objectives[45].

- **Encourage employees not only to *consume* but also to *produce and share* know-how** in their industry. By actively helping to advance knowledge in their team's domain – for example, by contributing content to conferences or organizing round-table discussions – they can also encourage others inside and outside the organization to share new resources and know-how in return.

THINGS TO AVOID

- **Planning with 100% capacity.** This may result in talent erosion, exhaustion, and burnout among key people in the team and organization. Even if a team devotes itself exclusively to project work, it will not be able to spend all its time completing the project. As a result, it will probably feel overloaded and start to miss deadlines. As a rule of thumb, it is better to plan with 80% capacity, in order to allow some margin for meetings, emails, sick days, or whatever else might cut into project time.

- **Inefficiencies and lack of agility in resource and talent allocation.** Most people resist any changes in organizational design, because they fear the reorganization's possible impact on them, their work habits, and their career. But this resistance is itself a risk factor, because their teams are likely to get locked into old practices and processes that have become obsolete. Our fast-changing VUCA context requires organizations to use resources in an agile way, reshuffle them constantly, and adopt new technologies swiftly.

- **Focusing solely on the skills that someone needs for a given role or function** instead of developing their *employability*. People have an intrinsic motivation to learn, grow, and acquire new skills through their work, and developing *transferable skills* will make them more resilient and secure when roles and projects change. Leaders who focus too narrowly on execution may aim exclusively to achieve organizational goals and fail to understand that learning is an integral part of achieving results.

- **Cutting your people development budget.** This sends a bad signal to teams, and will soon hurt your organization's morale, productivity, and performance. Talent development should be seen as a strategic *investment* and not a cost. Being too "mean" with people development may turn out to be more expensive in the long run, because you will need to acquire new skills from outside your organization.

- **Making the acquisition of new skills exclusively an individual goal.** A major part of an organization's performance is driven by teams making efficient use of their *collective* skills and know-how. Organizations that use personal development plans to nurture individual talent should consider introducing broader team development plans that look at the resources, skills, and know-how required to ensure optimal team performance.

---

[45]Britt Andreatta, "Creating a Culture of Learning in 6 Steps," Linkedin Learning, 2020, https://learning.linkedin.com/content/dam/me/learning/EMW/lil-guide-creating-culture-learning-6-Steps.pdf.

CUSTOMER EXPERIENCE

WHY IT MATTERS

Customer experience is vitally important to any organization. When a customer interacts with a company – for example, by navigating its website, using chat support, or exploring products and services – they end up forming an opinion of the overall experience. That in turn drives their perception – good or bad – of your organization and the services you deliver. Fortunately, a growing number of teams nowadays are starting to think in terms of service level and customer experience, including in the public sector. All teams should be clear as to who will benefit from the new products, services, and solutions that they are working hard to deliver. Does your team know who those end users are, and how to ensure that they will have an optimal experience?

THINGS TO DO

● **Know your customers,** and make sure your team has them in mind with every business decision it makes. Your team should be 100% clear on who your customers are, and why, when, and how they buy. It should know their budgets, needs, objectives, aspirations, expectations, pain points, and motivations. Instead of "studying" your customers, create opportunities to interact directly with them, and ask your team to go through the customer experience themselves so that they can assess it at first hand.

- **Develop a detailed map of your customers' journey,** and understand what factors make for a great experience along the way. Think about how you ideally want your customers to feel when they interact with your organization. Once you have established your version of the best customer experience, define your service level at each point of interaction and focus your efforts on delivering it.

- **Remember that the devil lies in the details,** and be mindful of all facets of your products and services. Every aspect of every customer's interaction with your organization adds to the overall customer experience. This includes timely delivery, reliability, product and service quality, how prompt, willing, and courteous your teams are in providing customer support, and the design and user-friendliness of your organization's website.

- **Continuously enhance the overall customer experience.** Take time to conduct process analysis, continuous process improvement, and root-cause analysis in order to improve your service. Develop creative ways to generate quantitative and qualitative feedback on customer satisfaction. Use indicators such as the Net Promoter Score, service level, and customer ratings, and translate them into actionable items that the team can influence.

- **Correct mistakes when they happen.** Successful teams know how to rectify errors with customers. When these teams notice a mistake, they proactively reach out to their customers, own up to the mistake in an empathetic and sincere manner, formulate a strategic response, execute it quickly, and apologize on behalf of the organization. Once the situation is back on track, they follow up internally to understand exactly what happened and why, and how they can avoid similar problems in the future.

THINGS TO AVOID

- **Having only one team dedicated to customer service.** Instead, aim to create a customer-centric culture across the organization. All employees should feel empowered to improve the customer experience and to act as ambassadors for your organization's products and services.

- **Over-automation at the expense of direct contact with your customers.** This can create a disconnect between your team and the people who buy its products and services. Customers appreciate personalized interactions, and prefer them to receiving bulk emails and having to navigate automated processes and frustrating phone trees.

- **Alienating your customers.** This might sound obvious, but I sometimes hear teams speak badly or arrogantly about their customers. In the worst cases, teams don't care about their customers, dehumanize them, or even regard them as a common enemy. Disrespecting or criticizing your customers, either in their presence or behind their back, is an absolute no-go.

- **Being reactive and dealing with customer service only in the back end.** Instead, think about how to enhance your service and delight customers at the front end, so that you can avoid complaints or problems later on. For example, ask everyone in your teams to take customer calls on a regular basis, and/or incorporate customer-service goals into their compensation and bonus structures.

- **Thinking that you know better than your customers.** Do what *they tell you* they want, not what you think they want. If you have good customer data, then use it! Get rid of predefined scripts for handling customer calls, and teach listening skills throughout the organization, especially to customer-service representatives.

DEPENDABILITY & TEAMWORK

WHY IT MATTERS

Almost every professional activity involves some form of *teamwork*, and it is essential that teams learn how to work together to accomplish common goals. Unfortunately, many fail to do so effectively, which leads to negative consequences. Working as a team can be complicated. The difference between working in a group and true teamwork lies in the level of interdependence and dependability among team members. High-performance teamwork requires – among other things – mutual trust, respect, and accountability, and interdependent work on common objectives.

THINGS TO DO

● **Create a team contract around "trust and dependability."** To collaborate effectively, teams need to find ways to coordinate each other's inputs swiftly and reliably. To help them do that, set group norms (a "contract") regarding what accountability, dependability, and mutual trust mean in the team. Everyone should know how to act and communicate in case they need help with an individual task on which the whole team depends.

- **Find efficient ways to engage in high-performance teamwork.** Activities such as brainstorming and coordination meetings may require the whole team, while other tasks are best done individually or in subgroups. Make sure you find the best way to engage all team members while making productive use of their time and resources. This requires structure and efficient coordination mechanisms.

- **Be inclusive and encourage diversity.** One of the great benefits of teamwork is that it brings together diverse skills, work methods, ideas, points of view, personal and professional backgrounds, ways of resolving issues, and communication styles. Inclusive teams always take a constructive approach to diversity, tactfully express different viewpoints, and build upon each other's inputs through helpful, not destructive, criticism.

- **Create opportunities to do real work together.** Instead of just having team meetings, organize fun and meaningful occasions for the group to engage in true teamwork through shared goals and projects, and problem-solving initiatives. Job-sharing and job shadowing can also be powerful ways to reinforce dependability and teamwork.

- **Offer spontaneous help to co-workers.** Everyone needs a hand now and then, and high dependability and teamwork imply that team members will readily assist each other when required. This could involve reviewing an important report before a colleague sends it out, or postponing a coffee break in order to take care of something for a co-worker who needs to complete an urgent task.

THINGS TO AVOID

- **Becoming overdependent and hyper-cohesive,** or slowing down individual initiatives because they have to be validated by the whole group. This blocks leadership at all levels within the team and is counterproductive. Avoid systematically wanting to resolve situations through teamwork; sometimes an individual contribution can be more effective.

- **Blaming others when they don't deliver – choose empathy instead.** Everyone can have a bad day, including you, so always put yourself in the other person's shoes. Be aware that team members might be facing complicated or distressing personal or family situations. Try to understand how your colleagues feel, or why they might have acted in a certain way, and then address the situation accordingly.

- **Criticizing others behind their backs.** Be sincere with your team. If something seems wrong with the group, or if you don't agree with one of their proposals, then say so, either to the entire team or to a specific person. Sincerity is the basis for all good relationships, including at work.

- **Communicating team successes in terms of "me" rather than "we."** It is not fair to claim credit for great teamwork without mentioning key contributors and praising those who actually did the job. Teams should speak with one voice, and encourage co-workers to share the stage and deliver joint project presentations.

- **Letting extroverts dominate the team.** Communication is as much about listening as talking. But in most teams, some people do too much or all of the talking, and don't listen enough. This is an easy trap to fall into, and most of us are guilty of it from time to time. All too often, I see the quiet person in a team beginning to understand a problem and trying to tell the rest of the group that they have the answer. But because they are quiet or shy or junior or new, and because the more dominant, senior, or vocal members of the team aren't listening, they give up. The team eventually gets to the solution, but it could have done so much quicker if it had better listening skills – and also if the quiet person had spoken up more confidently.

LEARNING, GROWTH, PROGRESS

WHY IT MATTERS

If you want to build a culture of learning, growth, and progress, then you need to embrace failure[46]. Learning and failing are inherently linked, so a positive and vibrant learning environment requires a culture in which people feel safe taking risks and making mistakes[47]. People and teams need to stay curious and even foolish; it saddens me when I see teams that have lost their inner drive and intrinsic motivation to learn and grow. When people are encouraged to take risks and don't fear failure, teams become transformed into incredible learning labs. The 70-20-10 framework for learning and development suggests that 70% of our learning comes from **experience** gained from day-to-day tasks, challenging assignments, and practice, 20% from **exposure** to different forms of collaboration and informal co-operative and coaching interactions with others, and only 10% from formal **education** via structured coursework and training programs. In other words, 90% of all learning opportunities arise from working in teams. Continuous learning plays an important role in boosting people's *employability*, and teams that provide a strong learning environment are better positioned to attract, develop, and retain great talent.

THINGS TO DO

● **Frame work as a series of learning opportunities.** Behind every challenge is an opportunity for growth and learning. Make sure your team sees through the fog and captures these opportunities while performing their current tasks. Instill a growth mindset across the organization by explaining that everyone's talents can be improved through practice.

[46]"Want to Build a Culture of Learning? You Need to Embrace Failure," https://learning.linkedin.com/blog/learning-thought-leadership/want-to-build-a-culture-of-learning--you-need-to-embrace-failure.

[47]Francesca Gino and Bradley Staats, "Why Organizations Don't Learn," Harvard Business Review, November 1, 2015, https://hbr.org/2015/11/why-organizations-dont-learn.

- **Encourage risk taking and tolerate "mistakes."** In a learning environment, there is no such thing as making mistakes. Learning is a trial-and-error process, and we need to feel safe in order to stretch into our vulnerability zone. Leaders should therefore encourage co-workers to take (appropriate) risks, try out new ideas, build prototypes, and develop proofs of concepts. See your team as a form of Fab Lab where people are free to experiment and unlock their creativity. Above all, provide support as team members move out of their comfort zone, and make sure to destigmatize failure.

- **Spend dedicated quality time with each team member.** Encourage them to cultivate their strengths, and discuss and plan their individual development needs. Consider potential when hiring and promoting, and make learning a normal and valued activity. Remember: to encourage learning, you need to allow time for it. Publicly praise team members who have taken the time to learn new skills, and recognize their additional know-how in a personal development plan that keeps track of their learning path.

- **Institute systematic project reviews with your team.** Whether you win or lose, your team must take the time to analyze why. Just as sports coaches and players debrief their performance right after a game, you should meet with your team after each important event or activity to discuss four key questions: What did we plan to do? What actually happened? Why did it happen? What are we going to do differently/better next time?

- **Share important learnings to inspire others within and beyond your team.** For example, your team could post cards on a dedicated "wall of learning," and review them regularly to help identify key insights. Encourage your team to learn from both successes and failures, because what they initially thought were failures may contain more lessons. A wall of learning will also make your insights visible to others who pass by your office, and thus stimulate their own learning and growth.

THINGS TO AVOID

- **The *fundamental attribution error.*** People commonly attribute their successes to hard work, brilliance, and skill rather than luck, but they blame their failures on bad fortune. This phenomenon, which psychologists call *attribution error/bias*[48], strongly hinders learning. In fact, unless people recognize that failure can result from their own actions, they do not learn from their mistakes.

- **Over-confidence bias.** Success increases our self-assurance. So does an overinflated ego. Faith in ourselves is a good thing, of course, but too much of it can make us believe that we don't need to change anything. To keep learning, we must have the humility to acknowledge our own weaknesses and errors.

- **Impostor syndrome.** People experiencing this phenomenon remain convinced that they are less capable than others and don't deserve all they have achieved, despite external evidence of their competence. Don't let your team and co-workers incorrectly attribute their success to luck, or undervalue their skills and talents.

- **Excessive workplace norms and procedures.** Having too many internal organizational rules may strongly inhibit new learning. Newcomers entering such an environment may decide to conform to the established status quo, thus limiting what they can bring to the organization.

- **The productivism trap.** Most organizational cultures value action more than reflection. But most of our "aha moments" that lead to insightful learning occur when we get out of our normal flow of activities. So, make sure you give your team some time and bandwidth to pause, step back, and reflect.

---

[48]Francesca Gino and Gary P. Pisano, "Why Leaders Don't Learn from Success," Harvard Business Review, April 1, 2011, https://hbr.org/2011/04/why-leaders-dont-learn-from-success.

ENTHUSIASM & POSITIVE ATTITUDE TOWARD CHANGE

WHY IT MATTERS

Whether an organization is planning a transformative change or is unexpectedly presented with a disruptive challenge, having a common approach to managing change can help it adapt better to the shifting environment. In today's VUCA context, it makes a big difference when teams have a positive attitude toward change. Being enthusiastic and able to see the opportunities is a powerful way to channel the team's energy. This requires leaders and teams to develop and model specific skills and ways of thinking so that the right mindset and energy diffuse within the group.

THINGS TO DO

● **Educate people about change.** Organizations need to create a common culture and systematically train people in change management. Nowadays, leaders must learn how to manage the processes, systems, structures, employee responsibilities, and overall morale during times of transition. Teams and leaders should also develop a shared vocabulary and understanding of the emotions that many people experience during the different phases of a transition.

● **Develop a clear communication plan** to be implemented before, during, and after the period of change. It is essential to anticipate in advance which forms of communication will take place at different times. Teams and organizations that operate transparently and provide information before, during, and after a transition will greatly reduce resistance to change.

- **Ask the organization's leadership to participate actively in the change.** Leaders cannot expect teams to adopt change if they are not fully involved in the transition themselves. They need to stay active and visible throughout the change cycle, not just during the initial phase. To get more leverage, C-level and executive teams should identify and sponsor key people who can champion change across the organization and lead by example.

- **Create a community** that includes both change promoters and people who are impacted by change. People resist change when it happens to them. When they are part of it, they can see how they are impacted and how to influence the process. One of the first things leaders need to do during transitions is to identify key stakeholders – both individuals and groups – and establish ways to engage with them early and often.

- **Work with change-management specialists throughout the transition process.** Your change-management team should consider involving external experts in the field. Specialized consultants can play a pivotal role by contributing their expertise and insights regarding change in different organizational contexts.

THINGS TO AVOID

- **Ignoring the root causes of change resistance.** Leaders often make the mistake of assuming that teams resist change because they are disengaged or difficult. In the majority of cases, people resist change because they are not convinced by it or have underlying fears. Leaders need to find out what the real sources of resistance are, and take action to deal with those. They should welcome resistance, and use it to generate a genuine debate that can help to address some of the team's caveats regarding the change project.

- **Failing to request or incorporate teams' real-time feedback** as you implement change. Leaders who don't adjust their plan based on their team's ongoing feedback during the roll-out phase may become too dogmatic and bullying as they push the change through. When instituting change, leaders must constantly measure its real-time effects, seek feedback on these, and be open to amending their plan to achieve the desired outcomes.

- **Dealing with change only through your lenses.** Teams need to handle change in a way that speaks to the different personalities of their members. Be mindful of personality types when developing your strategy and rolling out your change initiative. Inspirers may love the change and push you for more, while observers will be more cautious and are likely to question your rationale thoroughly before buying in. Shapers will step in and want to drive efficient decision-making and implementation, while coordinators will favor consultation and achieving consensus within the team before moving ahead.

- **Not framing the "Why."** Many leaders tell their teams what needs to change and how they will make it happen, but forget to outline the reason for the change. They should explain the rationale and frame it in the wider context of the organization's purpose, mission, and vision. Otherwise, the need for change risks being poorly understood, potentially creating a strong disconnect with a team's purpose and values.

- **Failing to acknowledge that losses and grief are part of change.** Emotions such as fear, anger, and sadness are natural in a change process. Expecting teams to accept change immediately without dealing with those feelings is a sure recipe for failure. People's reactions to major change go through successive phases, similar to the stages of grief. Understand that buy-in is gradual, and support your team in each phase.

INSPIRING GOALS: SELF & TEAM

WHY THEY MATTER

Goals are a double-edged sword[49]. They are certainly important for leveraging a team's energy and ramping up its motivation and productivity[50]. But some popular goal-setting techniques that may work well with individuals are not suitable for managing teams' collective performance, and therefore should be avoided. If not properly managed, the goal-setting process can cause a lot of frustration, reinforce a silo mentality, and even sometimes induce counterproductive behavior. Goals should be inspirational and framed in the context of a larger team purpose. Leaders must also make sure that individual and collective goals act in synergy to reinforce teamwork and cooperation rather than fueling destructive competition among co-workers.

THINGS TO DO

● **Start by setting goals for your team.** Know what you want to achieve and how your wider team goals will benefit the organization. These objectives need to motivate your team, fit individual roles, and be aligned with company aims. Everyone should be working toward the same outcome and understand how their work is contributing to the big picture. Create overarching collective goals that act as a glue for the team by reinforcing teamwork, synergies, mutual support, and cooperation.

● **Break down team goals into individual ones.** Once you have determined what your team wants to achieve, give people the autonomy to develop their own subsidiary goals based on their respective roles and functions. Team members should be able to determine key initiatives and goals that will support the group's broader objectives.

[49]"Dick Grote, 3 Popular Goal-Setting Techniques Managers Should Avoid," https://hbr.org/2017/01/3-popular-goal-setting-techniques-managers-should-avoid.

[50]"Robert H. Schaffer, Demand Better Results—And Get Them, " https://hbr.org/1991/03/demand-better-results-and-get-them.

- **Be transparent.** Make sure that both collective and individual objectives are clear to the team. This will help colleagues to be aligned and have a common focus, rather than trying to outperform each other. All project- or team-related objectives should be clearly communicated within the team so that people can come together as a more effective and collaborative unit.

- **Approach goal-setting as a partnership.** Recognize that performance planning is a collaborative process, not a solo activity. Use a participative approach, where you set goals based on each other's areas of responsibility, expectations in the role, and what you collectively want to see in terms of performance.

- **Understand how the Pygmalion[51] effect influences your goals…and your success.** Numerous studies show that people's performance will rise or fall to the level their superiors believe them capable of. You should therefore have high expectations for your team, and communicate these accordingly. Be aware of how you (and the Pygmalion effect) can influence your team's success, and use this understanding to benefit everyone.

THINGS TO AVOID

- **Organizational stiffness.** Organizations that lack dynamic processes may become too rigid and fail to adjust their goals in response to important changes in their environment. In the worst cases, this will result in a catch-22 where their goals end up working against them. Unfortunately, I have seen teams make choices that made no sense in order to achieve goals that had become irrelevant just so that they could tick a box in their next annual performance review.

- **Set-up-to-fail syndrome[52].** This is like having the Pygmalion effect work against you and your team's performance. Set-up-to-fail syndrome induces a negative feedback loop in which employees who are regarded as weak performers will sink in line with the low expectations their managers have of them. These expectations become self-fulfilling prophecies that undermine the individual's self-esteem and have negative side effects on the team's morale and performance.

- **Protect-your-bonus syndrome.** When bonus schemes are too tightly linked to individual goals, counterproductive behaviors may emerge. I know of cases where leaders set more conservative bonus-linked goals for themselves than they had assigned to their teams. This is a sure way to induce the wrong dynamics, diffuse an overly cautious mindset, and reduce trust in the organization's leadership.

- **Being unfair or unrealistic when setting or evaluating goals.** Nobody will be motivated by targets that don't really make sense. Anytime you set a goal, make sure that it meets the simple **SMART** criteria (**S**pecific, **M**easurable, **A**ttainable, **R**elevant, and **T**ime-bound). Better still, take the **SMARTIES** approach, and ask whether an objective is also Inspirational and Ethical, and whether your team can achieve it with a Smile :-)

- **Neglecting behavioral goals.** When setting goals with their teams, many leaders focus too much on what they want to achieve together and fail to set objectives regarding *how* they want to work. You should also set development goals that encourage your team to adopt the behaviors, activities, and actions needed to achieve the results you want.

---

[51] J. Sterling Livingston, Pygmalion in Management (Harvard Business Review Press, 2009).

[52] Jean-François Manzoni and Jean-Louis Barsoux, The Set-Up-To-Fail Syndrome: How Good Managers Cause Great People to Fail (Boston, Mass: Harvard Business Review Press, 2002).

COMMUNICATION TOOLS & PLATFORMS

WHY THEY MATTER

Rapid communication is essential to good team coordination and optimal performance. Possibly the single most effective way to improve interpersonal communication in the workplace is to instill a sense of trust among your team members. Within the team, swift coordination requires effectively combining in-person meetings with the virtual formats now available to most organizations. Finally, the team needs to establish optimal ways of engaging with key internal and external stakeholders on a regular basis. Most importantly, it needs to stay in close contact with its customers, including by taking advantage of new digital technologies and social media platforms.

THINGS TO DO

● **Have an open-door policy,** and invite everyone in the team to ask questions, voice concerns, and pitch ideas at any time. Keeping the doors of communication open builds trust and accelerates communication, enabling the team to address challenges quickly as they arise instead of waiting for the weekly team meeting.

● **Organize communications training.** This can be highly effective for improving group communication. Communications training doesn't cover only basic conversational skills. Depending on the topic, teams could also work on their presentation skills, and learn how to use oral, written, and digital communication more effectively to improve coordination and performance.

- **Ensure best fit.** Different situations require different forms of communication. For projects where team members are working remotely, a video conference is an excellent way to keep everyone up to date regarding progress and milestones. Face-to-face meetings are often the best method of communication for interactive team workshops involving brainstorming, process mapping, and root-cause analysis.

- **Use a project or team collaboration platform to improve coordination**. Most teams are turning to cloud-based solutions, and for good reason. Cloud-based tools promote transparency, enabling team members to track their progress, collaborate, review and comment on project details, and check due dates. Having a single streamlined system also greatly reduces the volume of emails.

- **Go digital and leverage social media.** Value the know-how that digital natives and millennials can offer to your team. Create reverse-mentoring initiatives where younger co-workers can coach older team members on smart ways to communicate and collaborate in a digital workplace. This includes using video and social media for internal and external team communication.

THINGS TO AVOID

- **Lack of transparency.** If team members feel that you are keeping secrets from them, any trust you might have built goes right out of the window. Although sensitive information should of course be handled as such, you should be open and honest with your team, and reassure them that they can be the same with you. Being authentic and transparent will also go a long way toward building mutual trust and positive relationships with your stakeholders and customers.

- **Lagging behind modern communication tools.** Teams that don't take advantage of mobile solutions and apps may not always have instant access to up-to-date information. As a result, they might be too slow or inefficient, or make bad decisions. These days, most project-management software solutions offer a mobile app for team members to stay on top of the latest developments.

- **Using too many communication platforms.** Spreading your team's interactions across numerous apps may lead to confusion and chaos. To communicate effectively as a team, you must choose exactly which platforms you will use and when, and for what purpose. Reduce the number of tools that you use, and make sure they give your team what it needs to operate effectively.

- **Failing to set group communication guidelines.** If you communicate too much, or without clear intent, you risk generating more noise than signal in a digital space that is already overloaded with constant information sharing. What might seem like the right amount of communication to one person may be far too much or too little for another. Establish clear communication guidelines that define the team's expectations regarding reply times, working hours, and the use of different apps and channels.

- **Team disconnects.** Paradoxically, overuse of modern digital tools can kill true dialogue and deeper human-to-human communication in your team. Make sure that you give your team time and space to engage in *relational* as well as *transactional* communication.

STAKEHOLDER & RISK MANAGEMENT

WHY IT MATTERS

Teams must constantly observe their operating environment, identify key organizational and individual stakeholders, and monitor potential threats and risks. They have to assess the group's vulnerability to specific risks, based on their likelihood and potential impact, and develop a strategy to reduce exposure to these. Wise teams manage risks and stakeholders simultaneously. These activities are closely related, and both are critical to the success of any project, program, or activity.

THINGS TO DO

● **Use a combination of tools and methods** to drive your reflection, structure information, and prioritize actions. These could include brainstorming, SWOT analysis, risk-assessment grids, stakeholder-analysis matrices, event-chain methodologies, and the use of specialized market-related statistical tools for financial assets.

● **Document all identified risks in a risk register.** This should contain information about each risk, including its nature, probability, likely impact, mitigation measures, owner, and status. These details are often displayed in a grid or a table.

● **Create a power/interest grid of stakeholders.** This tool enables you to map stakeholders into four quadrants, and defines how you should interact with and influence them (see opposite).

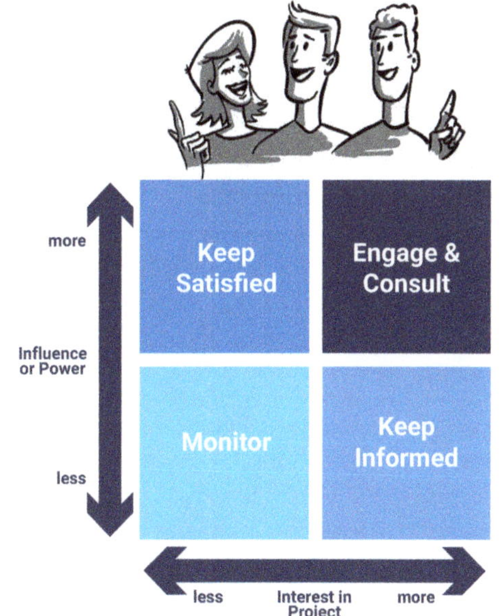

● **Establish a stakeholder communication plan** to clarify what you will inform them about, and when. This could cover project status updates, achievements, risks and opportunities, scope changes, and project delays. Be realistic in what you communicate and promise, and build trust with your stakeholders.

● **Approach stakeholder and risk management proactively.** Make it one of the team's priorities to review changes regularly, and follow up on your action plan accordingly. Don't do this just to tick the box and then leave the documents in your drawer until the next compliance audit.

THINGS TO AVOID

● **Restricting this activity to the leadership cockpit.** First, you won't leverage collective intelligence in performing your risk analysis. Second, team members may not feel accountable, empowered, or legitimate enough to communicate with key stakeholders.

● **"Improvements" that end up amplifying risks.** Teams often overlook the risks inherent in operational excellence and lean management. Be aware that pushing for operational efficiency and waste reduction can eventually lead to the removal of critical roles, people, processes, and inventory, leaving your organization highly vulnerable and without back-ups.

● **Neglecting what you should *not* do** as part of your risk-management strategy. Actions are celebrated more than inaction, but smart teams think about how they can reduce certain risks by avoiding certain steps. Deliberately choosing not to do something is often a more powerful risk-management strategy, because it enables you to lower some risks without introducing new ones.

● **Neglecting the human factor** and other psychological aspects when dealing with risks and stakeholders. Different stakeholders may view the same event in different ways, depending on the situation and their psychological risk tolerance. By over-focusing on risk mathematics, you might exclude important information from your risk scenario.

● **Systematically using past events to predict the future** or design risk-mitigation strategies. Instead, teams should use current (not past) tools and information to develop strategies for counteracting impacts from possible future risk events.

CLEAR ROLES & PROCESSES

WHY THEY MATTER

As Tammy Erickson[53] rightly says, "you need clear structure and well-defined interdependent roles in order to best leverage the strengths of those on your team." Having clear roles and responsibilities within the group allows you to recruit the right people with the required expertise. It makes for better teamwork, collaboration, and sharing, because each employee knows what is expected of them. And it reduces the potential for misunderstandings and conflicts, especially those that are related to authority. These benefits, combined with clearly defined processes, will help to avoid redundancy and overlaps and will make teams more effective.

THINGS TO DO

● **Clearly identify the type of roles** you need in your team. Remember also that smaller teams are usually more effective than larger groups. To paraphrase Albert Einstein, *teams* should be made as simple as possible, but not simpler. So, limit the number of roles in the team as far as you can.

● **Ask your teams to invest time at the start of their collaboration** to establish who will do what until individual roles and responsibilities are clearly defined and well understood. Each member's role should be clear before a team jumps into action.

---

[53]Tammy Erickson, "The Biggest Mistake You (Probably) Make with Teams,
" Harvard Business Review, April 5, 2012,
https://hbr.org/2012/04/the-biggest-mistake-you-probab.

- **Clarify roles and accountabilities.** Ask teams to create a list of all key processes and tasks. For each one, they should clearly identify who will do the work, and who will ultimately be accountable. A powerful way to do this is by using a **RASCI** responsibility-assignment matrix[54], which defines who is **R**esponsible, **A**ccountable, **S**upporting, **C**onsulted, or **I**nformed.

- **Make a visual chart** of how your team interfaces with the rest of the organization. Use it to analyze how the different roles within the team are connected or interrelated. Perform a gap analysis to see what other roles or expertise you might need. What functions are lacking, and in which departments? This will allow you to add positions that you now realize you need, while removing those that your processes or operations no longer require.

- **Encourage your team to create flow charts** for your most important business processes. Then, use process-improvement methodologies to remove bottlenecks, increase efficiency, and strengthen your teamwork. Choose the operational-excellence tools that best support your needs, whether Six Sigma, Lean, Kaizen, Hoshin, or one of the alternatives.

THINGS TO AVOID

- **Letting a political agenda determine your team's composition.** You will end up having too many functions represented or being forced to recruit the wrong people to fill the roles in your team. Either way, the team will be less effective.

- **Being too vague on the expectations and accountabilities** for each role. Individual roles are useless by themselves if they are not linked to an accountability or RASCI matrix that clearly describes how each role contributes to completing tasks and deliverables. For an organization to work effectively, a RASCI matrix should be established for each cross-functional or departmental project or process.

- **Using inappropriate methods and processes when making critical decisions.** Although a participative approach involving consensus or voting works well in certain situations, process-improvement or business decisions should be based on fact, not popular opinion. In those cases, define the criteria against which you will evaluate options or ideas before making a decision. If there is more than one attractive option, use the data when choosing between them.

- **Not allowing time for reflection and process improvement.** Most management teams want a continuous improvement culture but don't allocate resources to develop it. In particular, they often perceive team retreats and workshops as less legitimate than "production" time. Frequently, however, successful completion of a goal depends 80% on preparation and only 20% on execution.

- **Failing to anticipate and structure handovers.** Internal transitions are inevitable in any organization. Improper or problematic handovers frequently result in friction, greatly reducing everyone's efficiency and effectiveness.

---

[54]Gerardus Blokdyk, RACI Matrix A Complete Guide - 2020 Edition (5STARCooks, 2019).

WORKPLACE DESIGN & ERGONOMICS

WHY IT MATTERS

This team sustainability driver is not just about desks and chairs. Well-designed and ergonomically attractive workplaces can transform an organization's culture and employee experience by encouraging interaction, reinforcing a sense of community, and spurring exploration and participation. Workplace design critically influences the way that teams think, feel, and work together. In the long term, well-planned offices help to reduce sick leave linked to back pain and other musculoskeletal problems, and help organizations to engage and retain talented employees.

THINGS TO DO

● **Create modern office spaces** that stimulate individual and collective creativity and effectiveness. I am especially interested in the concept of *biophilic design*[55], which seeks to apply our instinctive bond with nature and natural surroundings to create better office spaces. Such designs emphasize natural light, live indoor plants, quiet working spaces, outdoor views of nature, and bright colors, for example.

● **Invest in ergonomic furniture** and give team members the flexibility and options to customize their workspace, including their desk, chair, keyboard, and mouse. This gives a clear signal that you value your team, and makes it more likely that they will stay with the organization for longer and do their best work. Ergonomic work stations also greatly reduce the risk of employee injuries and decreased productivity.

[55]Stephen R. Kellert, Judith Heerwagen, and Martin Mador, *Biophilic Design: The Theory, Science and Practice of Bringing Buildings to Life*, 1st edition (Hoboken, N.J: Wiley, 2013).

• **Design modular office spaces** that balance private and public areas. Some activities require more isolation, peace, and quiet so that people can do focused work, while other situations call for more social interaction with colleagues, visitors, and customers. A modular office space offers something for everyone, minimizes interruptions, and enhances overall productivity.

• **Offer flexible working arrangements.** These can include flex time, which allows team members to manage their work and personal commitments more easily, as well as remote-work options such as home offices or co-working hubs.

• **Minimize physical risks in the workplace** and make sure that your organization complies with the latest health and safety standards.

THINGS TO AVOID

• **Office environments with major defects or disturbances.** These may include a lack of natural light, excessive artificial light or glare (which can cause ocular fatigue), dry air, bad smells, and loud noise.

• **Clutter.** A messy workspace will hinder your team's performance and focus and send the wrong signal to co-workers, visitors, and customers. Keeping your workplace clean and free of obstacles can also reduce the risk of people injuring themselves by tripping or falling.

• **Regarding ergonomics and workplace design purely as a cost** instead of an investment. Badly designed workplaces can generate huge costs by causing employees to develop musculoskeletal disorders such as tendonitis, lower back pain, carpal tunnel syndrome, chronic headaches, and migraines. In most cases, these will far exceed the typical budget for establishing an ergonomic workplace.

• **Prolonged sitting and non-ergonomic workstations,** which can create or aggravate lower-back-pain symptoms. To help prevent such problems, start by asking an ergonomic specialist to guide your choice of office equipment. Then inform, train, and coach team members regarding ergonomics, and check their individual workplace set-ups. In addition, create a dynamic and energizing work culture that encourages people to regularly break up the monotony of sitting and promotes mobility, activity, and recovery throughout the day. Team members should feel free to stand, lie down, have walking meetings, do regular physical stretches, and use focus and relaxation rooms.

• **Not taking steps to protect your team's health and well-being,** and discouraging your staff from reporting early symptoms of possible physical problems. We may live in a society where we are expected to stay silent about everyday aches and pains, but in many countries the employer is liable for any workplace-related health and safety issues.

WORK-LIFE & ENERGY MANAGEMENT

WHY IT MATTERS

Personal energy management[56] used to be seen as having nothing to do with work. But in the last decade organizations have made a major shift and acknowledged that managing our personal energy has a profound effect on well-being, resilience, and productivity. Modern organizations also manage energy at a collective level. In their 2011 book *Fully Charged*[57], Heike Bruch and Bernd Vogel developed the following "energy matrix" that defines four states depending on the quality and intensity of an organization's energy:

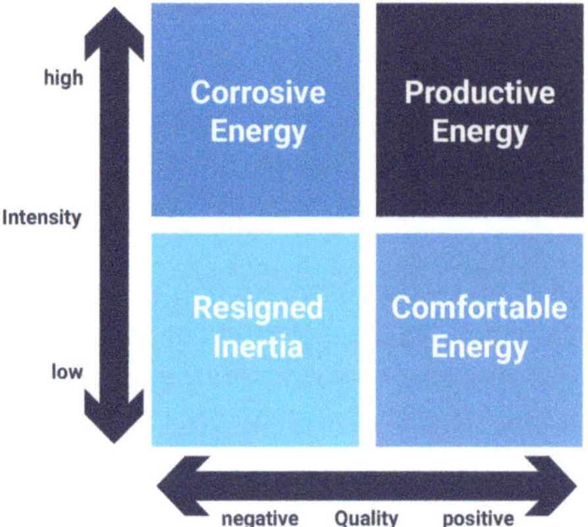

Achieving and sustaining a "productive energy" state will have a tremendous positive effect on both performance and well-being at an organizational, team, and individual level.

THINGS TO DO

● **Create a team culture** in which energy management is not only a personal dimension, but is also discussed and managed *collectively*. The whole team needs to be aware of where everyone stands, so that they can support each other, leverage the team's energy, and enable efficient teamwork.

---

[56]"Tony Schwartz and Catherine McCarthy Manage Your Energy, Not Your Time," http://hbr.org/2007/10/manage-your-energy-not-your-time; Tony Schwartz, Be Excellent at Anything: Four Changes to Get More out of Work and Life (London: Simon & Schuster, 2011).

[57]Heike Bruch and Bernd Vogel, Fully Charged: How Great Leaders Boost Their Organization's Energy and Ignite High Performance (Boston, Mass.: Harvard Business Review Press, 2011).

- **Consider all dimensions of personal energy** – physical, mental, emotional, and spiritual. Propose a range of activities to support these holistically in your team members, including nutrition and hydration, sleep, movement, meditation, and relaxation.

- **Make it fun for people to work and interact within the team.** Create occasions that promote a "high-positive" energy state, and lift your team's energy with laughter and optimism. Smiling is contagious, and a genuine smile spreads positivity and optimism. Sharing your passion can do wonders for raising a group's energy and inspiring great teamwork. Find novel, unexpected, and engaging ways for your team to interact and work together during meetings, workshops, and events.

- **Offer dedicated quiet areas** for people to focus, regenerate, and recover during the day. These spaces should be safe harbors where team members can recharge their batteries in a serene and peaceful setting. Spending time in such "low-positive" energy states contributes greatly to preventing stress, exhaustion, and burnout, increases concentration, and reduces injuries.

- **Offer flexible work schemes** that include options for how to use both paid and non-paid time off. These could include part-time work contracts, vacations, parental leave, and sabbaticals.

THINGS TO AVOID

- **Creating a culture that values only "high-positive" energy states** characterized by physiological arousal, activation of the sympathetic branch of the autonomic nervous system, and the fight-or-flight response. This fails to acknowledge the equal importance of "low-positive" energy states that enable physiological recovery, activation of the parasympathetic network, and the rest-and-digest response. You don't ask a marathon runner to run all the time, because efficient recovery is key to their performance. Likewise, understanding the role of *passive recovery* in the workplace is essential to renewing individual and team energy and maintaining long-term physical and psychological well-being.

- **Stigmatizing relaxation spaces.** Some organizations design nice modern offices with relaxation areas – but then no one dares to take advantage of them. People should be able to use those spaces without feeling that they will be judged or criticized for being lazy. Organizations and leaders should value passive recovery as a smart activity, and see it as integral to responsible and sustainable engagement, productivity, and effectiveness.

- **Promoting internal initiatives regarding work-life balance and energy management but not modeling those behaviors.** Senior executives who continue sending emails 24/7, systematically traveling for work on weekends, and not taking vacations create dissonance within the organization. This gives rise to a loyalty and authority conflict, because team members may feel safer following their leaders' behaviors than adhering to those being promoted through the well-being initiative.

- **Letting "high-negative" energy states deplete a team's energy.** Frustration, anger, or anxiety can induce chronic stress and fatigue, and negatively impact teamwork. External support may be required to help teams vent those emotions, overcome underlying frustrations, resolve potential conflicts, and find new ways to channel this energy creatively and constructively.

- **Institutional taboos regarding exhaustion and burnout.** Such situations inevitably arise in all organizations from time to time. Ignoring them creates an illusion of invulnerability and risks fueling a culture of denial. Instead, organizations should acknowledge their shared responsibility and seek to provide care, support, and resources to the individuals and teams affected in order to help them recover and reconnect.

RECOGNITION & REWARD

WHY IT MATTERS

The whole point of recognizing and rewarding employees is to encourage initiative and creativity across the organization. In today's increasingly agile and collaborative workplace, employees want frequent feedback, open communication, and opportunities to work with their peers. Many organizations are therefore replacing traditional annual evaluation systems with real-time, personalized employee feedback and kudos to acknowledge significant achievements. But this is not an easy task, and badly implemented recognition and reward systems can end up doing more harm than good.

THINGS TO DO

● **Complement annual performance reviews with a more dynamic approach** that incorporates frequent real-time feedback, open communication, and coaching. Seek to create a culture of continuous improvement that includes meaningful recognition of a person's achievements alongside constructive criticism to foster their further personal development and growth.

● **Empower everyone to contribute to 360° feedback across the organization.** This includes peer-to-peer, bottom-up, and top-down recognition. Feedback should be meaningful, personal, and immediate. For example, "spot rewards" – small tokens of appreciation given frequently and spontaneously by one colleague to another – can be a highly effective and fun way to recognize valuable contributions and strengthen bonds within a team.

- **Turn managers into coaches.** Today's team members don't see team or project leaders as experts in the way their predecessors did. Instead, they look to their managers for coaching and mentorship, and find purpose through constantly learning and growing on the job.

- **Find out how to motivate your team members.** Individuals in a diverse team are driven by different things. Ask people what motivates them most, and develop a range of ways to recognize and reward them. Be creative, and vary your approach to match individual needs. For example, consider giving thank-you notes, verbal praise, anniversary or birthday presents, cash or gift cards, tickets to an experience, stock options, or time off.

- **Organize small company-funded events** like barbecues or office parties that are dedicated to face-to-face interactions, presentations of rewards by one team member to another, and public recognition of individual and collective achievements. Make them special team moments that reinforce your organization's core values. Such events can give your co-workers an opportunity to express gratitude to each other on special occasions such as birthdays, work anniversaries, project completions, and welcome days.

THINGS TO AVOID

- **Excessive use of contests and competitive reward programs.** Over time, such initiatives create a pool of disappointed non-winners, which erodes morale and engagement and can be counterproductive for the organization.

- **Turning performance management into a bureaucratic, rules-based process** that exists as an end in itself rather than actually shaping performance. Employee evaluation schemes that just provide negative feedback once a year are even worse. Instead, team members need ongoing performance development, so that they know when they are moving in the right direction and how to make a positive change.

- **Making rewards all about money,** rather than acts of recognition. To forge a deeper commitment among team members, leaders need to go beyond material rewards and provide other forms of recognition. These can include praise from management, opportunities to lead or participate in interesting new projects, career-development possibilities, and training and learning programs.

- **Focusing too narrowly on hard goals** such as sales targets, success rates, or Net Promoter Scores. Your recognition and reward schemes should aim to reinforce your organization's culture and values (soft goals), which are harder to measure than performance-related deliverables and outcomes (hard goals). Linking rewards directly to these core values ensures that your reward and recognition strategy really supports your company culture, rather than just acting as another incentive for hard work.

- **Being unfair.** Fairness is critical to keeping teams motivated. Both academic and practitioner research suggest that managers' behaviors affect not only employees' health and well-being, but also their level of engagement[58]. A study[59] from the UK's Chartered Institute of Personnel and Development identified managers' ability to remain open, fair, and consistent as the number one management competency influencing employees' sustainable engagement. So, make sure that rewards appear equal and are based on a clear and logical decision-making process, and communicate this clearly to your team.

[58]Rachel Lewis and Emma Donaldson-Feilder, "Managing For Sustainable Employee Engagement - Guidance For Employers And Managers" (Chartered Institute of Personnel and Development (CIPD, London), 2012), https://www.cipd.co.uk/Images/managing-for-sustainable-employee-engagement-guidance-for-employers-and-managers_2012_tcm18-10753.pdf.

[59]Rachel Lewis, Emma Donaldson-Feilder, and Kate Godfree, "Developing Managers to Manage Sustainable Employee Engagement, Health and Well-Being" (Chartered Institute of Personnel and Development (CIPD, London), 2017), https://www.cipd.co.uk/Images/developing-managers-to-manage-sustainable-employee-engagement-health-and-well-being_2017_tcm18-18364.pdf.

INNOVATION & VALUE CREATION

WHY IT MATTERS

An organization's capacity to innovate and create value is intimately linked to its overall purpose: to create and deliver value in an efficient, sustainable, and cost-effective way. Ideally, this process should encompass all stakeholders along the value chain and also consider the benefits for the organization's wider environment and ecosystem. On a spiritual level, meanwhile, innovation is the expression of our creative talents and a powerful way to honor our life force.

THINGS TO DO

● **Always remember that you are aiming to create value for your customers and stakeholders.** Before starting to work on innovations, make sure that you thoroughly understand your customers' main activities, what "pains" they are trying to avoid (such as undesired costs or situations, negative emotions, or unwanted risks), and what "gains" (their ambitions and objectives) will ultimately make them happy[60]. During the innovation process, constantly ask yourself and your team, "How does this help us to create more value for our customers and stakeholders?"

● **Link your development activities to the organization's overall purpose and strategy.** It is easy to lose track of the bigger picture, so remind your teams regularly how their development efforts serve your organization's purpose and will make a difference for the end-users.

---

[60]Alexander Osterwalder et al., Value Proposition Design: How to Create Products and Services Customers Want, 1st edition (Hoboken: Wiley, 2014).

● **Use a mix of tools and methodologies** – both structured and unstructured – to stimulate your teams' creativity. For example, brainstorming or free-association techniques can work well in the ideation phases. A more structured approach such as the Business Model Canvas[61] developed by Alex Osterwalder and Yves Pigneur can then help you to build an integrated map of your team's value proposition and how it relates to your stakeholders' and customers' needs.

● **Use a prototyping approach** to rapidly bring new ideas and concepts to the market, gain experience, and gather feedback for further development. Tools that use a build-measure-learn feedback loop, such as Eric Ries's Lean Startup[62] model, will enable you to test new products or services quickly in order to make sure that you are investing in something your customers and stakeholders want.

● **Allocate resources appropriately.** Evaluate your human and financial assets and use them smartly, in areas where they have the most potential and that support your strategy. Balance risks and potential returns. For example, many organizations have a 70-20-10 principle according to which they allocate 70% of their resources to core initiatives, 20% to adjacent businesses, and the remaining 10% to transformational initiatives that focus on creating something completely new and out-of-the-box.

THINGS TO AVOID

● **Thinking that innovation means only product innovation.** In *Ten Types of Innovation*[63], Larry Keeley and his co-authors show how innovation and value creation can occur in many separate but interrelated dimensions, including business models and the supply chain.

● **Relying exclusively on the R&D department to come up with innovative ideas.** A successful innovation strategy relies on interdisciplinary teams gathering inputs from all the areas that influence the customer experience, including business models, products, services, sales, marketing, and the supply chain.

● **Creating a culture that encourages people to play safe and avoid risk, or that punishes failure.** Almost every successful organizational or commercial initiative encountered a setback somewhere along the way. But in too many organizations today, working on something that "fails" still carries a significant stigma, and maybe even a career risk.

● **Asking teams to generate ideas without creating mechanisms to do something with them.** This results in a long list of ideas that never go anywhere, which significantly demotivates teams and fuels organizational cynicism.

● **Thinking that innovative ideas emerge only from *cognition* and not from *intuition and experimentation.*** Organizations should reflect on the various ways to stimulate individual and collective creativity, and provide space, equipment, and materials for people to build, try, and experiment with new things. Most innovations emerge not in a meeting room but through trials, prototyping, and serious play.

● **Basing your innovation strategy solely on customer feedback.** Customers are crucial of course, but you should aim to balance their inputs with your vision. Chasing hundreds of different opinions will eventually slow you down, and you may have valuable insights of your own to feed into the innovation process.

---

[61]Osterwalder and Pigneur, Business Model Generation.

[62]Eric Ries, The Lean Startup: How Today's Entrepreneurs Use Continuous Innovation to Create Radically Successful Businesses (London: Penguin Books Ltd, 2011).

[63]Larry Keeley et al., Ten Types of Innovation: The Discipline of Building Breakthroughs, 1st edition (Hoboken, NJ: Wiley, 2013).

STRATEGY, ROADMAP, & PRIORITIES

WHY THEY MATTER

In today's VUCA world, organizations need to revisit the way they deal with strategy. A clear, viable strategy is still one of a team's most important assets: it sets out the long-term aspirations of the organization, how stakeholder value can be created, and what needs to be done to achieve this. However, strategy development and execution is becoming more dynamic, agile, and context-centric. Organizations that maintain an overly rigid approach to strategy management risk being disrupted out of their industry by rapid changes in their environment.

THINGS TO DO

● **Engage and mobilize key stakeholders,** including employees, customers, board members, advisory panels, governments, partners, and external consultants. This is vital in order to secure their commitment and support and avoid the problems of stakeholder politics. Their inputs can help you to develop superior insights on customer needs, market trends, and other big changes in your organization's wider context. Invest time to explore those issues, and make sure you fully understand them before developing a new strategy.

● **Use a modular, scenario-based approach to develop and test strategic options,** assess risks, and choose a strategy. Make sure your stakeholders and teams have a shared understanding of the organization's strategy before moving into the execution phase.

- **Be agile in executing your chosen strategy.** Regularly review and update your strategy, roadmap, and priorities in line with the latest changes in your environment. Swiftly communicate any adjustments to your stakeholders within and outside the organization.

- **Summarize your strategy in a simple, clear, visual roadmap.** A one-page, high-level roadmap will be far more effective in mobilizing people around a new strategy than a complicated and detailed Gantt chart. Keeping the plan short and simple will ensure that everyone in the organization can read, understand, and implement it.

- **Make strategy execution real-time and collaborative.** Compile all the key elements of your strategic roadmap into a collaborative digital platform. The latest generation of specialized software[64] for critical decision-making enables real-time mapping of your context, the factors at stake, and the associated risks, and tracks follow-ups of your action streams.

THINGS TO AVOID

- **Relying on assumptions or gut feelings in developing your strategy.** With the rise of the Internet of Things (IoT), more data is available today than ever before. This includes real-time and evidence-based feedback on customers' use of interconnected devices and services. If you have detailed, high-quality data, then use it to generate new knowledge and insights that can help refine your strategy. Teams should seek to base their strategy on as many facts and data as they can capture.

- **Letting only a few people (sometimes just external consultants) develop the strategy before rolling it out.** Instead, take a collaborative and participative approach and ask teams for their input. You will not only leverage collective intelligence and create a better plan, but also secure teams' buy-in early on, making future implementation much easier.

- **Self-satisfaction and failing to challenge last year's plan.** Don't be strategically complacent. Even if you have had a great year and your overarching objectives remain exactly the same, you still need to assess them in terms of the wider organizational context to ensure that you don't risk getting left behind.

- **Developing a plan that is disconnected from your organization's current reality.** Review your team's skills, resources, and capabilities (both human and financial) and make sure you have the budget or funding to deliver your plan – including by hiring new talent and investing in new systems. Your strategy should be explicit about how you are going to bridge the gaps.

- **Being too attached to or rigid with your plan.** Many organizations are too slow to change their strategic course when change is required. By contrast, successful teams are quick at making iterations, and set up regular review and learning cycles to adjust their strategic direction. They also use a combination of tools to monitor progress and get feedback during the implementation phase, including metrics, goals, milestones, KPIs, and dashboards.

---

[64]Marco Mancesti, "A management model specifically designed for crisis situations," Gerositus, 2020, https://www.gerositus.com/.

PSYCHOLOGICAL SAFETY & TRUST

WHY IT MATTERS

Being immersed in a highly complex, uncertain, and ever-changing environment can trigger unpleasant feelings of anxiety, insecurity, and fear in people. A powerful way for leaders to mitigate such emotions is to develop a strong feeling of safety, a secure base, and a circle of trust within both themselves and the team. Companies that have a trusting work environment perform better – and that kind of organizational culture is increasingly important in the modern economy, as Simon Sinek explained in a famous TED talk[65]. As Harvard professor Amy Edmondson points out[66], building psychological safety and trust with your team isn't about being nice. Rather, the aim is to give honest feedback, openly admit mistakes, be curious, and learn from each other.

THINGS TO DO

● **Create a safe space within the team** where people can share their thoughts, fears, doubts, vulnerabilities, personal feelings, experiences, and mistakes, and be willing to learn from one another.

● **Be honest and transparent** in the way you share information within the team. The more visibility into the future that people have, the better. Sharing information openly with your team also builds trust, and ensures that they are clear about the organization's plans, priorities, challenges and opportunities.

[65]Sinek, Why Good Leaders Make You Feel Safe.
[66]Edmondson, The Fearless Organization.

- **Foster an inclusive and participative approach** to problem-solving and decision-making. Enable everyone in the team to voice their ideas, provide inputs, and participate in decisions.

- **Have senior leaders connect and meet with teams regularly.** Executives should engage in open and honest dialogue about the organization's culture and the current levels of trust and fear. In addition, they should admit when the organization or they themselves make mistakes. Ask leaders to publicly demonstrate commitment to the organization, teams, and individuals.

- **Genuinely value and care for each other.** Leaders should check in regularly to see how everyone in the team is doing, what they are thinking, and what they would like to see happen. Be appreciative and inclusive. Acknowledge and praise each other's contributions and show how everyone brings value to the team.

THINGS TO AVOID

- **Not being present,** having poor social interactions, or maintaining emotional distance from the team. Cold and distant leaders can cause emotional frustration, stress, burnout, and disengagement within a team. In their book *Primal Leadership*[67], Daniel Goleman, Richard Boyatzis, and Annie McKee identified this as a characteristic trait of "dissonant leaders."

- **Sending mismatched signals.** One reason why we might feel uncomfortable with one of our colleagues in a team, at least at an unconscious level, is mismatched signals. That gut feeling stems from various factors, and signals cognitive dissonance resulting from conflicting attitudes, beliefs, or behaviors.

- **Dehumanizing each other.** Some leaders look at people as a pack and call them "our employees," "our staff," or "the headcount." They forget that behind the numbers are valuable colleagues, people, and human beings.

- **Creating a finger-pointing culture,** where people blame and shame each other for mistakes. Instead, encourage teams to view and analyze every mistake as a learning opportunity.

- **Applying infantilizing rules and methods,** or having too many internal guidelines and team policies. This will tend to encourage parent-child types of relationships in the workplace and reduce trust levels within the team.

---

[67]Prof Daniel Goleman PH D, Richard E. Boyatzis, and Annie McKee, Primal Leadership: Unleashing the Power of Emotional Intelligence (Boston, Massachusetts: Harvard Business Review Press, 2016).

CONFLICT & FEEDBACK MANAGEMENT

WHY IT MATTERS

Conflicts are an inherent part of teamwork. Every day, teams have to navigate their way through competing interests, clashing personalities, and time and resource constraints. When these multiple areas of tension are not properly managed, teams can become hostages to conflict[68]. To resolve conflicts effectively, all teams need to develop a mix of emotional intelligence, negotiation techniques, and feedback-management skills. But conflict is also key to growth, because it helps teams to challenge and move beyond the status quo. Experts in conflict management recommend that teams should even *seek* conflict in order to be more effective.

THINGS TO DO

● **Establish a common approach to dealing with conflict.** This should be based on group norms and a shared understanding of how your team manages serious disagreements. Help your team to develop rules, resolution mechanisms, and a common language regarding conflict.

● **Create a feedback culture and rituals,** and embed them into your team's routines. Plan dedicated sessions where team members can address conflicts openly – or "put the fish on the table," in IMD Professor George Kohlrieser's phrase. These sessions can take place on a one-to-one basis or in a group.

---

[68]Kohlrieser, Hostage at the Table.

- **Train your team in the use of Non-Violent Communication**[69]. Create opportunities to practice feedback dialogues using NVC principles or other feedback methodologies that provide structured dialogues, such as the Situation-Behavior-Feeling or the Needs-Impact-Desired Change methodology.

- **Use an adult-to-adult approach to manage conflict.** Tell your team about Eric Berne's model of Transactional Analysis[70] concerning human interactions, and especially how it applies to conflicts. Berne discusses Parent, Adult, and Child ego states, and highlights the risk of moving from Adult-Adult to Parent-Child (rebel or submissive) interactions during team conflicts.

- **Ask for help,** and work with a neutral third party who can assist you before a conflict escalates. This could be a mediator, ombudsperson, systemic work psychologist, or coach. He or she can act as an enabler to help you and your team identify and avoid common pitfalls that can arise during conflicts. For example, the pictogram below shows the dysfunctional interpersonal dynamics that take place between the oppressor/persecutor, victim, and rescuer roles in Karpman's Drama Triangle[71].

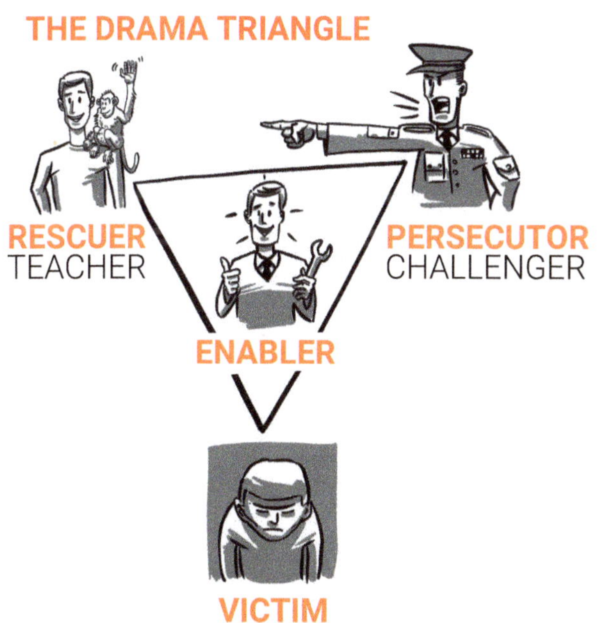

THINGS TO AVOID

- **Denying or ignoring conflict, or letting it sabotage your team**. Such behaviors are typical of dysfunctional teams[72]. Groups that avoid conflict and try to maintain *artificial harmony* will most likely underperform and remain stuck at an early stage of their development journey.

- **Conflict escalation.** If you are too passive in dealing with conflicts, they can reach a stage where they become destructive. Try to maintain a level of involvement that enables the conflict dialogue to produce a win-win resolution. This can help the team to generate new ideas and solutions, develop better mutual understanding, and strengthen feelings of empathy and interpersonal bonds.

- **Overexpressing power and authority when resolving conflicts.** This can lead to bullying, rudeness, heavy sarcasm, shouting, and even physical misbehaviors such as throwing objects in the workplace.

- **Underexpressing power and authority.** When exercised correctly, authority is a powerful catalyst driving accountability and efficient decision-making in groups. Leaders should use their authority appropriately to provide the clarity needed to resolve conflicts and reduce inefficiencies, confusion, and unnecessary work.

- **Being manipulative and inauthentic** during conflicts. Unfortunately, some leaders play favorites and pit staff against each other, talk negatively behind people's backs, and discredit their staff when talking to other managers. Others take a passive-aggressive approach, ignoring co-workers and not replying to their emailed or face-to-face questions.

[69]Marshall B. Rosenberg and Deepak Chopra, Nonviolent Communication: A Language of Life: Life-Changing Tools for Healthy Relationships, 3rd edition (Encinitas, CA: PuddleDancer Press, 2015).

[70]Eric Berne, Games People Play: The Psychology of Human Relationships (London: Penguin, 2010).

[71]Chris West, The Karpman Drama Triangle Explained: A Guide for Coaches, Managers, Trainers, Therapists – and Everybody Else (CWTK Publications, 2020).

[72]Lencioni, The Five Dysfunctions of a Team.

KEY LEARNINGS

Part V

1. Each of the 18 team sustainability drivers has its own **upsides** and **pitfalls**. Feel free to return regularly to Part V for inspiration on **how to apply them effectively with your team**.

2. Working with the 18 drivers can help your team to reach a **shared understanding** of its **development priorities**. **Regular follow-ups** will build momentum and keep you on track.

3. Although the drivers cover most areas of team development, I may have missed an extra dimension that is specific to your organization. Feel free to **add your own drivers** to this list!

Capture your own

 INSIGHTS

 ACTIONS

 THINGS TO SHARE

Final Thoughts

December 2020. As I finish writing this book, the COVID-19 pandemic has turned our health systems, economies, and societies upside down.

Let's reflect on this for a moment.

The minute virus that causes COVID-19 is just 65-125 nanometers in diameter, or more than a million times smaller than the size of our hands. The Earth's diameter, by contrast, is about 12,742 kilometers (7,918 miles).

Yet this tiny virus, which has a crown-like appearance under an electron microscope and is passively carried by its hosts, has disrupted the lives of more than 7.8 billion people.

The pandemic is thus a powerful reminder of the complexity, vulnerability, and interdependence inherent in the way we interact with our environment nowadays. Unfortunately, COVID-19 is just one of several major global crises that are likely to arise as a result of our dysfunctional environmental, social, and economic ecosystems.

That means organizations must rapidly acquire new skills to help teams build the resilience and agility they need to cope with recurrent disruptive change.

Over the last decade, organizations have developed a new vocabulary to help us make sense of an increasingly uncertain world. Instead of "change," we started to talk of transitions and transformations. Today, we increasingly think in terms of disruptions. So, which word will we use 5-10 years from now: chaos?

Every crisis creates an opportunity to pause, observe, and revisit the previous status quo. As we try to chart our way out of the pandemic, I hope that this book will in some way help leaders, teams, and organizations to recover from their recent traumas and navigate the journey ahead.

Some, of course, will try to return to "normal." But I hope that others will seize the opportunity to embrace a new paradigm for team and organizational development. In particular, I hope they will have the courage to shift their mindset and start building sustainable teams.

Acknowledgements

I thought that writing a book would be a lonely exercise, but I quickly realized that it is just another form of teamwork.

I feel humbled and grateful knowing that every idea in this book has been shaped in some way by people who have helped me in my life. I want to express my sincere thanks to many of them here.

First, to my mentor Marco Mancesti for his continuous support and friendship over more than 20 years. I always come out of our conversations feeling positively challenged and motivated to grow both professionally and personally. Marco's vision and valuable insights on leadership, strategy, and teams have helped to inspire the *sustainable teams* methodology and tools in this book.

Next, to Professor George Kohlrieser, because without him I would not be the person I am today. Working with George and his incredible team of coaches has become a strong part of my secure base. I was privileged to take part in his High Performance Leadership (HPL) program at IMD, which gave me the caring and daring I needed to dig into the past and make sense of my life. George and my HPL coaches Marie O'Hara and Andreas Neumann enlightened this journey through personal post-traumatic work. Together with my coaching supervisors Mireille Rosselet-Capt and Veronica Galli Iölster, they were instrumental in helping me heal my wounds, reconnect with the joy of life, and become a better leader.

To my dear colleagues, associates, and co-workers at Actitudes Coaching, whose insights into organizational psychology, systemics, neuroscience, and business and people development have nurtured our vision of what a diverse workplace can be. Thank you to Kallia Apazoglou, Peter Bakker, Ralph Bland, Anne-Laure Egger-Dormond, Bettina and David Greiner, Mark Guilbert, Arnold Helmig, Sabrina Huguenin, David Picard, Hanael Sfez, Nathalie Sofia, Cecilia Tarabusi, Hervé Tategrain, Maria Wilhelmsson, and last but not least Andrea Zahno.

To Richard Eames, who edited this book assiduously and with great insight. To David Picard for bringing an artistic dimension into this work through his design and illustrations. To Olivier Fischer, Cyril Lamblard, Marco Mancesti, and Frédéric Rivier, who spontaneously offered to review the manuscript and improved it significantly with their comments. And to Vincenzo Palatella, who kindly shared his experience in guiding me smoothly through the book-publishing labyrinth.

To my parents and sister. Your love and support as I was growing up have strongly influenced my personal values, education, and professional ethics. I learnt many of my early lessons about leadership and team dynamics from you, and these have since diffused into my work and this book.

To my wife Susan. Every day, I feel grateful for the act of synchronicity that made us enter each other's lives on the last Christmas Eve of the old millennium. Without your unconditional love and support, I would not be working in this field and writing this book today. More importantly, I would not be the husband, father, and man I am now.

I have been blessed with a network of friends too large to name here, so I will just mention a handful from the Swiss Federal Institute of Technology with whom I am still in touch today: Alex "The Boss" Gavric, Patrick Hauert, Alex Leutwiler, Vivian Stauffer, Didier Vuagniaux, and Urs Weber. Our lifelong friendship means a lot to me and is a valuable asset as we all navigate our way through life.

When I look back, many other people have played a pivotal role in different areas of my life. Their inputs have been and still are crucial to my success at key turning points in my personal and professional journey. I would therefore like to sincerely thank Ruedi, Isabel, and The Baumeler Clan, Barbara Bernath, Vincent Bourgeois, Stéphanie and Christophe Broggi-Tschann, Michel Chatelain, Andrea Collins, Nicolas Corsi, Céline Desmarais, Carole Dusonchet, Patrizia Feroleto, Jean-Pierre Fonta, Veronica Galli, Alain Gendre, Jean-Pierre Heiniger, Anne-Sophie Hofer, Catherine and Gaël Mangenot-Dorogi, Laila Merval-Gaedecke, Sonia Micello, Laurence Mottier, Marianne Niquille, Nathalie Nyffeler, Audrey Olivier-Muralt, Fabio Pasquali, Andrea Pfeifer, Giulia Polito, Jens Regelin, Nicole and Mathieu Rieder-Schärer, Nathalie Ritter, Dorothée Roessinger, Rosa Luisa Rossi, Pierre-Alain Ruffieux, Bernard Schmid, Carlo Serafini, Urs von Stockar, Elisabeth Svandberg, Xavier Tissière, Emmanuel Vallélian, Christophe Waeber, Jack Wood, and Dominique Wullschleger.

Finally, I want to express all my love and appreciation for my wonderful children Sofia, Felix, and Noémie. As you grow into young adults,

I hope this book will help to create a world where sustainable leadership, teams, and organizations are the new norm.

Bibliography

Andreatta, Britt. "Creating a Culture of Learning in 6 Steps." Linkedin Learning, 2020. https://learning.linkedin.com/content/dam/me/learning/EMW/lil-guide-creating-culture-learning-6-Steps.pdf.

Beer, Stafford. Diagnosing the System for Organizations. 1st edition. Chichester: Wiley, 1995.

Berne, Eric. Games People Play: The Psychology of Human Relationships. London: Penguin, 2010.

Blokdyk, Gerardus. RACI Matrix A Complete Guide - 2020 Edition. 5STARCooks, 2019.

Boynton, Andrew C, and Bill Fischer. Virtuoso Teams: The Extraordinary Stories of Extraordinary Teams. Harlow: Financial Times Prentice Hall, 2009.

Brown, Brené. Daring Greatly: How the Courage to Be Vulnerable Transforms the Way We Live, Love, Parent, and Lead. London: Portfolio Penguin, 2012.

Bruch, Heike, and Bernd Vogel. Fully Charged: How Great Leaders Boost Their Organization's Energy and Ignite High Performance. Boston, Mass.: Harvard Business Review Press, 2011.

Burnout… A Friend of a Friend's Problem | Frédéric Meuwly | TEDxSHMS, https://www.youtube.com/watch?v=T-TRTG7l1cV0.

"Circular Economy - UK, USA, Europe, Asia & South America - The Ellen MacArthur Foundation," https://www.ellenmacarthurfoundation.org/.

Covey, Stephen R. The 7 Habits of Highly Effective People: Powerful Lessons in Personal Change. Mango, 2016.

"Digital Adoption through COVID-19 and beyond | McKinsey," 2020. https://www.mckinsey.com/business-functions/mckinsey-digital/our-insights/the-covid-19-recovery-will-be-digital-a-plan-for-the-first-90-days.

Duhigg, Charles. The Power of Habit: Why We Do What We Do, and How to Change. William Heinemann Ltd, 2012.

Edmondson, Amy C. The Fearless Organization: Creating Psychological Safety in the Workplace for Learning, Innovation, and Growth. 1st edition. Hoboken, New Jersey: Wiley, 2018.

Eger, Dr Edith Eva. The Choice: Embrace the Possible. New York: Scribner, 2017.

Erickson, Tammy. "The Biggest Mistake You (Probably) Make with Teams." Harvard Business Review, April 5, 2012. https://hbr.org/2012/04/the-biggest-mistake-you-probab.

Ericsson, K. Anders, Ralf Krampe, and Clemens Tesch-Römer. "The Role of Deliberate Practice in the Acquisition of Expert Performance." Psychological Review 100 (July 1, 1993): 363–406. https://doi.org/10.1037//0033-295X.100.3.363.

Gino, Francesca, and Gary P. Pisano. "Why Leaders Don't Learn from Success." Harvard Business Review, April 1, 2011. https://hbr.org/2011/04/why-leaders-dont-learn-from-success.

Gino, Francesca, and Bradley Staats. "Why Organizations Don't Learn." Harvard Business Review, November 1, 2015. https://hbr.org/2015/11/why-organizations-dont-learn.

Goleman Daniel, Richard E. Boyatzis, and Annie McKee. Primal Leadership: Unleashing the Power of Emotional Intelligence. Boston, Massachusetts: Harvard Business Review Press, 2016.

Grote, Dick. "3 Popular Goal-Setting Techniques Managers Should Avoid," https://hbr.org/2017/01/3-popular-goal-setting-techniques-managers-should-avoid.

Hardy, Darren. The Compound Effect. Vanguard Press, 2012.

Harvard Business Review, John P. Kotter, W. Chan Kim, and Renée A. Mauborgne. HBR's 10 Must Reads on Change Management. 1st edition. Harvard Business Review Press, 2011.

Hawkins, Peter, and Eve Turner. Systemic Coaching: Delivering Value Beyond the Individual. 1st ed. Routledge, 2019.

Katz, Daniel. The Social Psychology of Organizations. 2nd edition. Wiley, 1978.

Keeley, Larry, Helen Walters, Ryan Pikkel, and Brian Quinn. Ten Types of Innovation: The Discipline of Building Breakthroughs. 1st edition. Hoboken, NJ: Wiley, 2013.

Kellert, Stephen R., Judith Heerwagen, and Martin Mador. Biophilic Design: The Theory, Science and Practice of Bringing Buildings to Life. 1st edition. Hoboken, NJ: Wiley, 2013.

Kohlrieser, George. Hostage at the Table: How Leaders Can Overcome Conflict, Influence Others, and Raise Performance. 1st ed. Jossey-Bass, 2007.

Kohlrieser, George, Susan Goldsworthy, and Duncan Coombe. Care to Dare: Unleashing Astonishing Potential Through Secure Base Leadership. 2nd ed. Jossey-Bass, 2012.

Laloux, Frederic, and Ken Wilber. Reinventing Organizations: A Guide to Creating Organizations Inspired by the Next Stage in Human Consciousness. 1st edition. Brussels: Nelson Parker, 2014.

Lencioni, Patrick. The Five Dysfunctions of a Team: A Leadership Fable. 1st edition. San Francisco: Jossey-Bass, 2002.

Lencioni, Patrick M. The Advantage: Why Organizational Health Trumps Everything Else In Business. John Wiley & Sons, 2012.

Lewis, Rachel, and Emma Donaldson-Feilder. "Managing For Sustainable Employee Engagement - Guidance For Employers And Managers." Chartered Institute of Personnel and Development (CIPD, London), 2012. https://www.cipd.co.uk/Images/managing-for-sustainable-employee-engagement-guidance-for-employers-and-managers_2012_tcm18-10753.pdf.

Lewis, Rachel, Emma Donaldson-Feilder, and Kate Godfree. "Developing Managers to Manage Sustainable Employee Engagement, Health and Well-Being." Chartered Institute of Personnel and Development (CIPD, London), 2017. https://www.cipd.co.uk/Images/developing-managers-to-manage-sustainable-employee-engagement-health-and-well-being_2017_tcm18-18364.pdf.

Livingston, J. Sterling. Pygmalion in Management. Harvard Business Review Press, 2009.

Mancesti, Marco. "The Disruption-Fit Leader and Why Companies Need Them to Survive." IMD business school. Accessed March 19, 2020. https://www.imd.org/research-knowledge/articles/the-disruption-fit-leader/.

Mancesti, Marco. "A management model specifically designed for crisis situations." Gerositus, 2020. https://www.gerositus.com/.

Manzoni, Jean-François, and Jean-Louis Barsoux. The Set-Up-To-Fail Syndrome: How Good Managers Cause Great People to Fail. Boston, Mass: Harvard Business Review Press, 2002.

Marquet, L. David, and Stephen R. Covey. Turn the Ship Around!: A True Story of Turning Followers into Leaders. 1st edition. New York: Portfolio, 2013.

McChrystal, Gen Stanley, Tantum Collins, David Silverman, and Chris Fussell. Team of Teams: New Rules of Engagement for a Complex World. 1st edition. New York, New York: Portfolio, 2015.

Miller, James Grier. Living Systems. Niwot, Colo: Univ Pr of Colorado, 1995.

Osterwalder, Alexander, and Yves Pigneur. Business Model Generation: A Handbook for Visionaries, Game Changers, and Challengers. 1st edition. Hoboken, NJ: John Wiley and Sons, 2010.

Osterwalder, Alexander, Yves Pigneur, Gregory Bernarda, Alan Smith, and Trish Papadakos. Value Proposition Design: How to Create Products and Services Customers Want. 1st edition. Hoboken: Wiley, 2014.

Piccard, Bertrand. Solar Impulse Foundation. 1000 profitable solutions for the environment, https://solarimpulse.com/.

Ries, Eric. The Lean Startup: How Today's Entrepreneurs Use Continuous Innovation to Create Radically Successful Businesses. London: Penguin Books Ltd, 2011.

Robertson, Brian J. Holacracy: The New Management System for a Rapidly Changing World. New York: Henry Holt and Co., 2015.

Rosenberg, Marshall B., and Deepak Chopra. Nonviolent Communication: A Language of Life: Life-Changing Tools for Healthy Relationships. 3rd edition. Encinitas, CA: PuddleDancer Press, 2015.

Schaffer, Robert H. "Demand Better Results—And Get Them," https://hbr.org/1991/03/demand-better-results-and-get-them.

Schwartz, Tony. Be Excellent at Anything: Four Changes to Get More out of Work and Life. London: Simon & Schuster, 2011.

Schwartz, Tony, and Catherine McCarthy. "Manage Your Energy, Not Your Time," http://hbr.org/2007/10/manage-your-energy-not-your-time.

Schwarz, Roger M. Smart Leaders, Smarter Teams: How You and Your Team Get Unstuck to Get Results. 1st edition. San Francisco, CA: Jossey-Bass, 2013.

Sibbet, David. "Process Models." Accessed March 18, 2020. https://davidsibbet.com/process-models/.

Sinek, Simon. Start with Why: How Great Leaders Inspire Everyone to Take Action. Reprint edition. New York, NY: Portfolio, 2011.

Sinek, Simon. Why Good Leaders Make You Feel Safe. https://www.ted.com/talks/simon_sinek_why_good_leaders_make_you_feel_safe.

Sustainable Development Knowledge Platform.https://sustainabledevelopment.un.org/.

"The Future of Work | Mobilizing Business Action to Shape a Future of Work That Enables People, Business and Societies to Thrive.," https://futureofwork.wbcsd.org/.

Tuckman, B. W. "Developmental Sequence in Small Groups." Psychological Bulletin 63 (June 1965): 384–99. https://doi.org/10.1037/h0022100.

Von Bertalanffy, Ludwig. General System Theory: Foundations, Development, Applications. Revised. New York: George Braziller Inc, 2015.

Vries Manfred F.r. R. Kets de "The 'Authentizotic' Organization: Creating Best Places to Work." SSRN Scholarly Paper. Rochester, NY: Social Science Research Network, April 25, 2018. https://doi.org/10.2139/ssrn.3168680.

Vries, Manfred F. R. Kets de. The Hedgehog Effect: The Secrets of Building High Performance Teams. John Wiley & Sons, 2011.

"Want to Build a Culture of Learning? You Need to Embrace Failure," https://learning.linkedin.com/blog/learning-thought-leadership/want-to-build-a-culture-of-learning--you-need-to-embrace-failure.

Webster, Ken, Dame Ellen MacArthur, and Walter Stahel. The Circular Economy: A Wealth of Flows. 2nd Edition. Cowes, Isle of Wight, United Kingdom: Ellen MacArthur Foundation Publishing, 2017.

West, Chris. The Karpman Drama Triangle Explained: A Guide for Coaches, Managers, Trainers, Therapists – and Everybody Else. CWTK Publications, 2020.

Wheatley, Margaret J. Leadership and the New Science: Discovering Order in a Chaotic World. 3rd Edition. San Francisco: Berrett-Koehler Publishers Inc., 2006.

"WHM Effectiveness Review - Gesundheitsförderung Schweiz." https://healthpromotion.ch/workplace-health-management/studien-wirkung-bgm/whm-effectiveness-review.html.

Yunus, Muhammad. Building Social Business: The New Kind of Capitalism That Serves Humanity's Most Pressing Needs. Reprint edition. New York, NY: PublicAffairs, 2011.

About the Author

Frederic Meuwly, Ph.D. is the founder and managing director of Actitudes Coaching, a management consulting firm specializing in executive team development and organizational health.

As a consultant and keynote speaker, he has worked with thousands of senior executives and team members in organizations ranging from established companies and high-tech start-ups to universities and non-profit entities.

To learn more about Frederic and the products and services his company offers, please visit
www.actitudescoaching.com

www.ingramcontent.com/pod-product-compliance
Lightning Source LLC
LaVergne TN
LVHW071524180726
843512LV00014B/1161